THE WARRIORS

Reflections on Men in Battle

J. GLENN GRAY

With a Foreword, 1970,
by the Author

Introduction by
Hannah Arendt

UNIVERSITY OF NEBRASKA PRESS
LINCOLN AND LONDON

TO URSULA, MY WIFE,
FORMERLY ONE OF "THE ENEMY"

♾

First Bison Books printing: 1998

Library of Congress Cataloging-in-Publication Data
Gray, J. Glenn (Jesse Glenn), 1913–1977.
The warriors: reflections on men in battle / J. Glenn Gray; with a new
foreword, 1970, by the author; introduction by Hannah Arendt.
p.   cm.
Originally published: 1st. ed. New York: Harcourt, Brace, 1959.
ISBN 0-8032-7076-3 (pbk.: alk. paper)
1. War.   2. World War, 1939–1945—Personal narratives, American.
I. Title.
U21.G75   1998
355.02—dc21
98-8030   CIP

Reprinted by arrangement with the author.

CONTENTS

"It is quite in keeping with man's curious intellectual history that the simplest and most important questions are those he asks least often."

—NORMAN ANGELL

INTRODUCTION

HANNAH ARENDT

Something strange and disquieting happened to this book when it was published seven years ago. As a rule, very good books don't go unnoticed, just as we hope that only very bad books end up on the junk piles in editorial offices. To be sure, almost everything imaginable can and does happen to the majority of printed matter which must fall between such extremes—neglect, *succes d'estime*, best-seller list; and since this could hardly be otherwise in view of the flood of publications which, year in and year out, deluge critics and readers alike, much depends upon this rule for the presence of a minimum of standards and intellectual integrity in the general climate of our culture. But exceptions prove the rule, and when we see that Glenn Gray's

The Warriors is among them, we can only pray that they may be rare. The book was almost entirely overlooked when it first appeared, and yet, by force of sheer availability on the market, it has acquired, slowly and surely, its own circle of not just admirers but lovers, a group of readers in very different walks of life who cherished it as a triumph of personal discovery and, perhaps for this very personal reason, began to think of its author in terms of affinity, closeness and affection, which are very rarely felt even in the presence of masterpieces. So let us console ourselves with the hope that such fraternal welcome, unmediated by critical and public opinion, awaits those authors who, for one reason or another, have not been sucked into the dubious mainstream of notoriety.

Moreover, with regard to this book, there is something oddly appropriate to its slow and intimate success. The author, an intelligence officer during the second World War, tells what he experienced and learnt during more than four years of battle and enemy occupation; and since this particular warrior, of whom a friend even then had "thought as *the soldier*," happened to be a philosopher (he received, ironically enough, his induction notice into the Army with the same mail that brought him his doctorate from Columbia University) it took him four-teen years of remembrance and reflection to understand and come to terms with what had happened in these four years. This much time was needed to learn "simplicity" and to unlearn "the simplification of abstract thinking," to become fluent in the art and the language of "concrete" thoughts and feelings, and thus to comprehend that both abstract notions and abstract emotions are not merely false to what actually happens but are viciously interconnected; for "abstract thinking is strictly comparable to the inhumanity of abstract emotions," the love and hatred of collectives—my own people, *the* enemy, especially in wartime, or, finally and in a mood of disillusionment, either hatred of or blind allegiance to "mankind collectively [which] is doubtless as predisposed to injustice as nations are."

Hence, the first lesson to be learned on the battlefield was that the closer you were to the enemy, the less did you hate him—"a civilian far removed from the battle area is nearly certain to be more bloodthirsty than the front-line soldier," unless, of course, the soldier happens to be a killer, and only pacifists who hold abstract notions and emotions about war will mistake the one for the other. Thus, "soldiers who cherished concrete emotions found the moral atmosphere at the front so much more endurable than in rear areas that they willingly accepted the greater strain and personal danger of combat." These soldiers became our author's spiritual brothers for they, too, would agree that Nietzsche was "surely right" when he wrote: " 'Rather perish than hate and fear, and twice rather perish than make oneself hated and feared.' " And the second lesson was that no ism, not nationalism and not even patriotism, no emotion in which men can be indoctrinated and then manipulated, but only comradeship, the "loyalty to the group is the essence of fighting morale." This self-taught concreteness, an unswerving fidelity to the real, as difficult to achieve for the philosopher, whose formal education had been abstract thought, as for the common run of men who indulge in no less abstract feelings and emotions, is the hallmark of this singularly earnest and beautiful book.

What must strike the reader to begin with in a book about war is its peculiar stillness, the softly reflecting tone of this voice that never teaches or preaches but tells in the greatest modesty what the author remembers. The remembrance begins on the first page; after fourteen years, Gray has begun to re-read his war journals and letters. This sets the scene. He finds

them "sad and laughable and strange" as they remind him of
Plato's description of the people in limbo at the end of *The
Republic*. But they also make him aware of how much he has
forgotten, of an "absence of continuity between those years and
what I have become," and now he is afraid "to continue to
forget" since such oblivion might indeed confirm "the deepest
fear of my war years ... that these happenings had no real
purpose," that they "might well signify nothing or nothing
much." This fear, he confesses, "is still with me." From which
we may conclude that he never forgot but that only now the time
had come to tell.

Surprisingly enough—as though he did not know how much
what he has to tell would go against the grain of fashionable
convictions and modern sensibilities in these matters—he begins
his tale with "the enduring appeals of battle:" the "confraternity of danger;" the "powerful fascination" of the "spectacular;" the "poignancy and intensity" of life in the face of
death, for "just as the bliss of erotic love is conditioned by its
transiency, so life is sweet because of the threats of death that
envelop it;" the "lightheartedness" that comes from being
"liberated from our individual impotence and [getting] drunk
with the power that union with our fellows brings," a feeling
akin to intense aesthetic pleasure when we are so absorbed by
its objects that our "ego deserts us" and we feel no longer "shut
up within the walls of the self and delivered over to the insuffi-
ciencies of the ego;" finally, the wondrous "compulsiveness" of
love in wartime when "it falls upon us 'like a mountain wind
upon an oak, shaking us leaf and bough,' in the striking simile
of the poet Sappho." Gray sums up these enduring appeals,
quoting General Robert E. Lee's remark, "It is well that war is
so terrible—we would grow too fond of it," in the word "ecstasy"
that occurs again and again; for what all these experiences have

in common is that men are literally standing, or rather thrown, outside their selves, whether their " 'I' passes insensibly into a 'we' " or they feel so much "part of this circling world", so much alive that, in seeming paradox, death no longer matters to them. It is easy to agree that erotic love is of such an ecstatic nature, but the point of the matter is that comradeship is too, and that friendship is not just a more intense form of comradeship but its very opposite: "While comradeship wants to break down the walls of self, friendship seeks to expand these walls and keep them intact. The one relationship is ecstatic, the other is wholly individual," the one is amoral (not immoral), the other guided by moral responsibility. But since all morality depends upon self-awareness, and hence a certain amount of self-love, self-sacrifice is inspired by comradeship rather than by friendship; for "friendship makes life doubly dear," and the "unendurable fear that grips friends on the battlefield is at the farthest remove from the recklessness of the soldier-killer" and of the "love for self-sacrifice" which, as we well know, can be aroused with equal ease for good and bad causes.

Re-reading the book, one is tempted to quote endlessly and thus deprive the reader of his own discoveries and the great pleasure that goes with them. On the surface of it, this is a book about *homo furens* and *homo sapiens,* but in fact it is about life and death, love, friendship, and comradeship, about courage and recklessness, about sensuality and the "surge of vitality", about "inhuman cruelty" and "superhuman kindness," not as stereotype opposites but as simultaneously present in the same person, (for "war compresses the greatest opposites into the smallest space and the shortest time," that is its greatest fascination), and at the end about conscience, the very opposite of ecstasy, since conscience means "to set oneself against others and with one stroke lose their comforting presence." To be sure, these are no more nor less than the elementary data of human existence but "unless human beings are pushed to the extreme, we are not so likely to confront simple and primal realities," or to reflect about them.

Opposition to war comes easy today and for Glenn Gray it is a matter of course. It did not need Hiroshima and Nagasaki nor the fact that even in World War II more civilians were killed than soldiers in combat to teach him "the ache of guilt" which to his great surprise has been almost totally neglected in contemporary novels that deal so freely with every other agony of combat. Among the great merits of the book is that it makes opposition to war forceful and convincing by not denying the realities and by not just warning us but making us understand why "there is in many today as great a fear of a sterile and unexciting peace as of a great war." And to make his point, he tells the story of a Frenchwoman whom he had known in the years of dangers and sufferings and then met again in peace and comfortable circumstance. She said: "Anything is better than to have nothing at all happen day after day. You know that I do not love war or want it to return. But at least it made me feel alive, as I have not felt alive before or since." Gray comments: "Peace exposed a void in them that war's excitement had enabled them to keep covered up," and he warns of the "emptiness within us," of the exultation of those who feel bound "to something greater than the self." Could boredom be more terrifying than all of war's terrors?

The book, in its undemonstrative subdued fashion, turns about a little episode that happened in the hills of the Apennines. There, not too far away from the front lines, he had encountered an old man, illiterate and apparently a hermit, who was peacefully smoking his pipe in the neighborhood of no living being except his donkey. The soldier was immediately welcomed beside him on the grass because it turned out that the old man was greatly mystified by the din and dust of battle which could be seen in the distance; he did not know that a war was going on. This was strange enough. But it was stranger that the two men, the soldier and the hermit, "began to talk at once of important things as naturally as if we knew one another well." Here our author was again confronted with "simple and primal realities," but now far away from the exultation of war and the extremities of battle, in "peaceableness and sanity," where the "familiar and the evident" seemed no longer remote because two men could share, outside, so to speak, of history, their concern about "the important questions: Who am I? Why am I? What is my function in life?" This was fraternity, and it was possible because one of them, the old man and hermit, was blessed with "the gift of simplicity" and the other, soldier and philosopher, had been stripped of his normal sophistications, of all that is subtly false in what we teach and learn. For this is what had happened: "The professors who had taught me philosophy and for whom I had had great respect and esteem became all at once puny in my imagination. . . . Even the great thinkers of Western civilization seemed suddenly to lose their stature and become only human beings. . . . Their wisdom was almost grotesquely inadequate for the occasion." No such wisdom could be expected from the illiterate peasant beside him on the grass; his company was not inadequate. Both were outside civilization, outside tradition and culture, the soldier because war had thrown him into one of those lonely foxholes with nothing to keep him company but "watching the stars at night," the hermit because it was "as though he had sprung from nature herself . . . her authentic child;" so the one had unlearnt and the other never possessed "the arrogance" that makes men "exaggerate the significance of the human story in relation to the rest of nature's household."

The book concludes as it should with reflections about "the future of war" and the prospects for "eternal peace." Rejecting optimism and pessimism as equally "irrelevant" and convinced that "peace will never occur as a consequence of weakness, exhaustion, or fear," he hopes that the day will come when the strong and the mighty—"a people distinguished by wars and victories," in the words of Nietzsche, quoted by the author—will " 'break the sword' " because they can afford to say "that men ought to choose death twice in preference to being feared and hated" and that "survival without integrity of conscience is worse than perishing outright." Nowhere perhaps than in these passages does one understand better that Glenn Gray's friend thought of him as *the soldier.* For they express but the last and, under today's circumstances, inevitable conclusions of the soldier's basic credo—that life is *not* the highest good.

New York, February, 1966

FOREWORD, 1970

Like many Americans I have been trying to come to terms with the peculiar horrors of the Vietnam war and the violence, chaos, and emotional perplexity these horrors have occasioned —or reflected—in our own land. In me they once more open up the intellectual wounds of World War II, which I had sought to heal by writing this book a decade ago. At the close of the present decade is there any reflection that might lessen an iota the mounting confusion in my own and other minds?

At that time I felt, more than understood, that "something is wrong, dreadfully wrong" with contemporary civilization. This feeling was a consequence of the character of total war in which terroristic bombing of cities and civilians became for the first time the rule. The culmination was the destruction of Nagasaki and Hiroshima with the most abstract of all death-dealing instruments.

In this book I tried to comprehend what the practice of total war did to man as warrior. For the warrior who slays an impersonal enemy has traditionally not been regarded as a criminal, a murderer. Yet in the era of total war the distinction becomes ever more blurred. And the dissociation in our lives between soldiering and civilian pursuits grows at the very period when distinguishing between combatants and noncombatants threatens to disappear altogether. As I now see it, in the 1950s this was the source of my emotional conviction that something was dreadfully awry in the contemporary world. Today few would dispute the fact that something has gone wrong, though exactly what it is eludes us.

A few months ago I got some intellectual insight into *what* is wrong by means of two unrelated experiences. At the University of Hawaii I heard a Japanese philosopher speak of "the monstrous character" of modern civilization. He was referring to Japan's adoption of Western science and technology, which has resulted in one of the highest gross national products in the world. At the same time Japan has become, according to him, the most godless nation of all, with no real motivations other than impulses for material goods and sex. His words were for me more impressive because I learned to know him, in a week's association, as no Cassandra bemoaning the loss of religious faith and indulging in reactionary nostalgia. Though a serious man, he was anything but gloomy. His lecture and discussion centered on the issue of whether men of the East or West can survive without any god or gods. And his answer to explicit questions about this was an unyielding No.

At the time I had just completed a review of Daniel Lang's painful account of "the incident of Hill 192," the subject of his *Casualties of War*, in which a veteran of Vietnam recounts to Lang why he resolved to report and bring before a court-martial the other members of his patrol, who in November, 1966, had abducted, raped, and then deliberately murdered a Vietnamese girl. While pondering his motivation for not participating in the crime and for undertaking the hazardous task of bringing his comrades to trial for it, this simple ex-soldier spoke the following to Lang:

We all figured we might be dead in the next minute, so what difference did it make what we did? But the longer I was over there, the more I became convinced that it was the other way around that counted—that because we might not be around much longer, we had to take extra care how we behaved. Anyway, that's what made me believe I was interested in religion. Another man might have called it something else, but the idea was simply that we had to answer for what we did. We had to answer to something, to someone —maybe just to ourselves.

With their words the Japanese professor and the Vietnam veteran brought something to a focus in me with which I had long been contending. Are these manifestations of our monstrous age a consequence of the death of all gods? What does it mean to attempt to live godlessly?

Answering the first question affirmatively, as my experience of the present decade prompts me to do, depends in great part on my interpretation of the second. When I wrote this book at the end of the last decade I already perceived one aspect of godlessness, namely, that remoteness from reality in warfare that I called abstraction.

Abstractness is illustrated once again in the furor occasioned by the Songmy massacre. To the usual judgment this deed seems far more of an atrocity than the actions of the pilots who bomb such hamlets from the sky or of the artillery men who lob in shells from a great distance. The reason given is that the infantrymen are brutalized by their deeds. Yet brutalization is hardly the worst that can happen to a man, for it can be healed in time and in circumstances of peaceful living. But the man who kills from a distance and without consciousness of the consequences of his deeds feels no need to answer to anyone or to himself. His is an unconscious depravity that can increase imperceptibly in civilian life. Dissociated from his deeds he can become far more monstrous than the infantry soldier or lower-echelon officer who occasionally goes beserk under battle strain. The "terrifyingly normal" men, who are ever in the vast majority, are those who make our age a monstrous one.

Now I understand better than I did that such normal men are everywhere. They need not be bombardiers or captains of artillery. The atrocities and "incidents" of Vietnam are hardly isolated occurrences and unrelated to the American or any other tradition. Despite the assurances of Administration officials to the contrary, reflection teaches a deeper truth, to wit, that such deeds are more or less a product of modern culture, which has increasingly grown godless.

What are the further implications of living godlessly? For one thing it implies forgetfulness of the encompassing world to which we are so totally bound, both as individuals and as a species. No longer do we feel answerable to this encompassing which is within us, as memory, imagination, and consciousness, or without us as soil and sun and air and water. We are forgetful of the fact that these latter are not simply things of our environment but natural powers and fibres of which we are made and which enable us to be sustained in existence every moment. They are verbs, not nouns, and the adverb "godlessly" qualifies these verbs, alas now in a negative sense.

Thoughtlessly we conceive nature as external environment. Thinking, and presumably remembering, too, is supposed to be "non-natural." But that which sustains us in being is surely as much these nonmaterial activities of thinking, remembering, creating as digesting, breathing, locomotion, and the like. Possibly they are not so different in kind, as perhaps our sciences will one day establish.

Such godless living means for another thing that our species fancies itself to be the purpose and goal of creation—perhaps not merely of our tiny earth but also of the inconceivable range and extent of the cosmos now that we have broken through earth's atmosphere. This suggests a forgetfulness of the most obvious fact of our mortality, that we are late-comers to creation and probably early departers. The dissociation of man as individual and species from the limitless backgrounds of his being is another quality which constitutes the monstrous character of contemporary civilization.

In curious ways conventional religionists illustrate such godlessness as surely as avowed atheists, if not more so. Too typically they abjure thinking man's backgrounds by clinging to a man-centered universe and fashioning god in our image. Putting emphasis on believing—which they equate with faith—they distrust contemporary insights and become atavistic in the worst sense. The god they seek is ever "the God of our Fathers," never of our children's children. Their religion seems to be little more than superstition and consolation. To them living godlessly would connote the denial of the physical existence of the Judaic or Christian god, always imagined as a Person and thought of in capital letters, someone to whom they pray when in dire straits or praise in good times. To speak of gods, as the Japanese philosopher did, would seem primitive to them, for everyone knows that monotheism is "higher" than polytheism. Few consider seriously that other world religions have their own god or gods, much less do they take seriously the obvious fact that the Jewish or Christian god is hardly the same god for different believers. Nor would they understand any better the simple, profound remark of the ex-soldier that "we had to answer to something, to someone—maybe just to ourselves."

If man's attempt to live without gods appears, in the harsh light of present realities, a failed attempt, is a reversal of our course possible? Some perplexed thinkers are persuaded that nothing can be done. They see our new technetronic culture as a destiny that must be lived out to the end. According to them, the problem of godlessness is not a moral crisis, not a failure of man, rather it is a withdrawal of the divinities from human view. Such withdrawal has been gradual, long in the making over the last centuries, and coincidental with the slow coming to dominance of man over external nature and its exploitation by him. Mind sundered from its fount and original habitat inevitably gives rise to subjectivistic ideologies in conflict with one another. These become the very shape and substance of present reality. To believe that we can change this fate through a moral reformation in any meaningful sense is to abide in illusion. The powers of history are superior to any willed determination of men, even of man.

I agree that moral reformation is hardly an appropriate response to the withdrawal of the sense of divinities in human existence. Religion is not morality; it is both more and less than morality. Yet I am unwilling to accept the conclusion that nothing can be "done" to alter our fate. Though a profound religious consciousness, of the sort I imply in this book, is not something willed or within our powers, it may nevertheless come over us when our true situation becomes sufficiently clear.

That is to say, the absent and hidden gods may reveal themselves once again when we are prepared for their coming. They are unlikely to come in the form of a revival of Judaism or Christianity, much less in the shape of a "foreign" religion like Zen Buddhism or others. They are likely to show themselves, if at all, in a new manner and form. Yet, as always in profound changes, the new is in so many respects "the oldest of the old." Such a recovery of religious faith would be a kind of self-recovery of our society. Hence it would surely be not without our doing though hardly within our control.

This way of thinking can scarcely help our nonplused citizens to come to terms with atrocities in Vietnam, assassinations of our public figures, and increasing violence on campuses and in cities of America and Europe. It certainly will not if we rest content with surface features and fail to give thought to the disappearance of the limitless backgrounds of human life. Only if we regain contact with the sources of our being in that nature within and about us will we be able to discover new road markers on the path ahead for the remainder of this century. Only those who have bridged some of the discontinuities in Western tradition will dare to think the radical new thoughts that set up these road markers.

I am far from the claim that the reflections on men in battle which compose this book are sufficiently profound to establish any markers. But I am confident that the struggle to comprehend my experience as a soldier in World War II provides a perspective on past and future that helps to reduce the discontinuities of the monstrous present.

J. GLENN GRAY

December, 1969

A NOTE TO THE READER

Since much of the material for this book is drawn from my experience in World War II, it is best to set down here a brief record of my military service. I was inducted into the Army as a private on May 8, 1941, having received my "greetings from the President" in the same mail that brought word from Columbia University that my doctorate in philosophy was conferred. On October 28, 1945, I was honorably discharged as a second lieutenant, a battlefield commission having been granted me in December 1944 at Strassburg, France. These four years of service covered nearly a year in an armored division, over a year in Washington, D.C., as an agent of the Counter Intelligence Corps, and not quite two years overseas in the European Theater of Operations. At the end of 1943, I was sent to Africa to join an infantry division en route to the Italian front. As a member of the counter-intelligence unit I participated in the Italian campaign, the invasion of southern France, and the campaign in middle Europe until the end of the war, being, in the process, attached successively to three infantry divisions. The responsibility of our unit was the safeguarding of troops against spies and saboteurs which the enemy might send across the front or leave behind among the civilian population.

The nature of our task demanded an unusual amount of freedom and mobility. Because we worked constantly with civilians in Italy, France, and Germany, it was possible to observe the effects of war on the native populations as well as on our own soldiers. An additional year in educational reconstruction after the close of the war gave me opportunity to observe postwar reactions in shattered Europe.

The book was largely written during a recent year in Germany, made possible for my family and me by generous fellowships from the Fulbright Commission and the Ford Foundation. This year of leisure afforded me a new chance for long talks about the war in the perspective of a decade with Germans from all walks of life. They ranged from General Hans Speidel, Rommel's former chief of staff, to Hitler Youth recruits of the last days of the war; from nonmilitary men and women, students, housewives, ministers, to survivors of the July 20 revolt against Hitler. Despite the fact that we had fought each other not long before, as individuals and nations, it was possible to discuss the past with little rancor or distrust, one of the most curious phenomena of human relations.

During this year, my reading in German war literature extended from von Clausewitz to contemporary novels, memoirs, letters, and personal accounts of World War II, much of it as yet unknown in America. For several years I have studied widely, if unsystematically, comparable writings of our own tradition and of Britain, France, and Russia. Though comparatively little of it is cited in the following pages, I should not want to minimize the effect of this reading in correcting and expanding my own experience of warfare. It is only because the intention and the aim of my book are so different that I was able to make little direct use of this literature, but I am no less indebted to it as background.

For critical reading of the manuscript and for friendly encouragement, I wish to express my gratitude to Mrs. Lillian McCue, Professor William Hochman, and Dr. Ellsworth Mason. Professors Frank Krutzke and Lewis Pino have been wise counselors in the practical matter of finding the proper publisher.

J. GLENN GRAY

Colorado College

THE WARRIORS

ONE

REMEMBERING

WAR

AND

FORGETFULNESS

Dear Fred: It has been long since I wrote you. I don't know how long, whether a week or three. The last weeks have been hard, filled with many bitter, hateful things and only a few short happy interludes. What a heritage the Nazis leave behind them! Sometimes I feel very old. What my eyes have seen! We have been a long time in the line and the picture at times seems never to change. Only the personalities are different. Joy and beauty have many different faces but brutality and hatred have but few. I have come to the extremity of knowing beyond all doubt that there is no other way for me to survive this period except the hard Christian way of finding the finer points in my associates and loving them for those characteristics. The bare cold, prophetic words of Auden,

We must love one another or die

have rung in my mind on several of these frigid, sleepless nights of late.

3

Perhaps even you cannot participate enough in this life over here to understand. You would have to see a fine, fine family broken, people you had learned to love, destroyed because of petty personal grudges. You would have to see people slapped and beaten because they might possibly be telling a lie or because certain sadistic impulses need to be satisfied. You would have to see old men and women on the roads with a few pitiful belongings in a driving rain, going they know not where, trying to find shelter and a little food in a scorched-earth area. Oh, you would have to see many things, Fred, to know why I should come to realize such a primitive truth as that I have only one alternative to death and that is to love, to care for people whom I, as a natural man, want to strike down.

The time may not be far off, if it is not already here, when millions of people will not want to live. It has been prophesied and the prophecy is a true one. Today I talked with a young attractive woman with three children who told me she did not care what happened to her. She wanted to die. There was no theatricality about her at all. She was not suffering from any physical illness and she was not hungry. Separation from her husband, bombing, living in cellars, no future—all of it had become too much for her. Always the same picture—immer das gleiche Bild.

But I find courage and strength from somewhere. I shall go on. Plato wrote of the wise man caught in an evil time who refuses to take part in the crimes of his fellow citizens and takes refuge behind a wall until the storm is past. Plato understood. But I am too deeply involved. Such a course is not possible for me any longer. So I am driven to the Christian way out. It is hard, yet there is great comfort in finding it. I sleep better now, and because I give love I find it oftener. You will not like such writing as this, yet I cannot write anything else at the moment. It is late and I am tired. . . .

December 9, 1944

After fourteen years it is a disquieting experience to read my war journals and letters like this one. Sad and laughable and

4

strange, so Plato described the behavior of the people in limbo at the end of *The Republic,* and this best expresses my present feelings. What had brought me to such a state of mind? And what significance can remembering it have in our present perilous world? The first question I can answer honestly, if not easily, by means of memory aided by my journals and by letters returned to me by a friend. The second has already occasioned much pondering, hesitation, and doubt, the end of which I cannot yet foresee.

This particular letter was written in Alsace, where fanatical SS troops had finally halted our division after its precipitous advance from the beaches of southern France. We had been committed to the front lines well over a hundred days without rest, and it is easy to recall how tired we were. The fierce resistance at the borders of Germany made our days nasty and dangerous. Almost worse were the recriminations and persecutions among the unfortunate Alsatians of those thought to be pro-German. Shopkeepers were changing their signs as well as their language from German to French after having done the reverse in 1939; political opinions were not so easily reversed in a vengeful atmosphere where nearly everyone was suspect. Moreover, we had just come into this area from the Vosges Mountains, from which the Germans withdrew only after they had set fire to everything in order to deprive us of all shelter in the menacing winter temperatures soon to come. As a consequence, the roads were filled with refugees of all ages and conditions. Loaded with what they could carry on their backs, on bicycles, or on carts, men, women, and children streamed to the rear.

It had not been very different in Italy, where my division had participated the previous spring in a similar race from Cassino to the Arno, a campaign so aptly described by

5

Churchill as "the fiery rake," except that this was a crueler climate and the rain that beat upon the refugees seemed more pitiless than in the south. There was another difference. Here we frequently met huge covered wagons drawn by steers or oxen and piled high with farm implements and cooking pots. On top of the gear under the canvas tops perched women and children while the men goaded the beasts in front and boys led the cows at the rear. Somehow these peasants had persuaded the Germans to let them salvage a portion of their possessions.

Inevitably, these conveyances reminded me of our American pioneers in the nineteenth century. Nothing else was similar, for, unlike pioneers, they had no destination. Their goal was behind them and there was no light in their faces. With an aching heart I reflected on this regression from pioneers to refugees and wondered if some future historian might not find these terms most characteristic of the nineteenth and twentieth centuries. There was something patently symbolical about the contrast, which I have not since been able to put from mind.

The enemy was cruel, it was clear, yet this did not trouble me as deeply as did our own cruelty. Indeed, their brutality made fighting the Germans much easier, whereas ours weakened the will and confused the intellect. Though the scales were not at all equal in this contest, I felt responsibility for ours much more than for theirs. And the effect was cumulative. It had begun before my division had even reached the front in Italy at the beginning of 1944. Bivouacked some thirty miles to the rear, I had watched hungry Italian women and children standing in February rains, holding crude cans with wire handles to collect leftover food from our mess. The American soldiers were generous, and it was easy to notice that more food than usual was left in the mess kits, to find its way into the eagerly extended cans of the thin and shivering civilians. Rarely did they eat it on the spot, however tempted; their dependents in the village nearby were evidently uppermost in their thoughts. Inexperienced and fearful in a strange land, higher headquarters soon put out stern orders that all garbage was to be buried forthwith. Then began the hideous spectacle of unwilling soldiers forced to push back the women and children while garbage cans of food were dumped in freshly dug pits. Other soldiers hastily shoveled the wet dirt over the meat, bread, and vegetables. To prevent scavenging at night, it became necessary to fetch dry earth and tramp the surface of the "sump" until it was packed. More than once we saw the despairing children and women break through the lines and scrabble in the rain and mud to rescue dirty pieces of food before the soldiers could seize them and push them away. "And though it wrenches my heart to see them," I wrote in my journal, "I soon grow accustomed to the sight and eat my fill. How hard is the heart of man!"

Could it have been I who witnessed this scene and wrote these words in this journal? My memory does not deceive me, and, if it did, the pages are before me. It is true that most of us did not want to behave in this way; in fact, the faces of these green troops registered utter disgust with such senseless orders. But we did not protest; we steeled ourselves, thinking, no doubt, that much worse sights were in store.

It would be superfluous, as well as too painful, to recall many of those worse sights. Because of its peculiar character, however, one other episode haunts my mind and may be briefly set down. It happened in southern France shortly after our invasion. One day an attractive French girl appeared at our temporary headquarters and confessed that she had worked for a time with the local Gestapo and now feared the revenge of the Maquis. The French security officer with whom I was working interrogated her calmly at some length and soon found out that she had been in love with the Gestapo captain in charge of this district and had been persuaded to aid him on occasion in his repressive measures against the Resistance. Since our unit had to move on almost at once, the French officer wrote a report of his interrogation for the civil authorities of the liberated city—and closed it with his recommendation that the girl be shot! On the way to the city jail with the girl, he picked up some pictures of his wife and children, which he had had developed in a local photography shop during our brief stay. After showing them to me for my comment and approval, he carried them to the girl in the car ahead. Ignorant of the fate he had decreed for her (and which would almost certainly be carried out at once under conditions at that time), the girl admired the family snapshots and the two of them laughed and joked for many minutes. Passers-by might easily have mistaken them for lovers.

There was little savagery or blood lust in this French officer. He did not hate the girl, so far as I could tell, though he hated her deeds. He would, in fact, have been quite willing to sleep with her the night before ordering her execution. When I remonstrated with him about such callousness, he made clear to me that he regarded himself as an army officer in a quite different way from himself as a human being. The two personalities could succeed each other with lightning rapidity, as I was to see on numerous occasions. As a human being, he was capable of kindness, even gentleness, and within limits he was just and honest. In his capacity of functionary, he could be brutal beyond measure without ever losing his outward amiability and poise. I observed precisely the same qualities in the Fascist and Nazi politicians and police with whom it was my fate to deal.

After months of this sort of experience, I began to detect with a kind of horror that I was becoming inured to cruelty and not above practicing it myself on occasion. In the spring of 1945 I find entries like the following in my journal:

. . . And as Spring comes and the days lengthen, and sunshine and warmth penetrate, one becomes aware what toll the winter has taken. Last Spring I saw in Italy the lush red fields of poppies, the death flower, and knew that mines lay beneath them. This Spring there are only the mines. So it is with our lives. The camouflage, beautiful if treacherous, is falling away and we are left with the ugly deadly surface. I grow bitter and sarcastic. Today I yelled at a character who had lied to me and took a certain pleasure in seeing the perspiration come to his face and his hands tremble. He knew the power I had over him. So do one's values become corrupted and conscience coarsened by this ordeal. But enough of this . . .

And a few months later, in a letter to my friend, I wrote:

One becomes incredibly hardened. Now I often despair of myself. I interrogate these "bastards," as we call them, sneeringly, insultingly, and sometimes take cold delight in their cringing. I have declared that if ever I find one who will say: "I am, I was, and will remain a National Socialist and you can like it or not," I will clasp his hand and cry: "At last I have found a brave and honest, if an evil, man. We don't want to arrest such a one as you." But I think I shall not find such a man. They are all as disgusting as the Fascists in Italy—all arrant cowards who say they were forced to do what they did, even if it was to enter the Party in 1928. From high to low—and I have had some big shots—the story is the same. I am tempted to think that the key to the whole rotten mess is lack of courage and fear. Cowards best understand the psychology of fear. That sentence explains much to me. Few

9

*of them have the courage to take their own lives, though the
fellows in the Detachment accuse me of losing my cases or solving
them by this route. I do not like such jokes, but on the other hand
I have not had a bad conscience about those who have "cheated"
me by that route. Oh, it is all a dirty, lousy business and I sometimes ask God why I have to be chosen for this particular work.*

Now I realize how tenuous were the links to my friends
and to my journal, which kept me integral and not too deeply
stained by the monstrous cruelty of war. Becoming a functionary is not entirely foreign to the nature of the majority
of us.

However overwhelmed by brutality and suffering I became
at times, they represent, after all, only one aspect of war. It
would be false to dwell solely on them and ignore other
features of war experience that are equally important. There
was also the intense nervous excitement of great moments, in
which even the dullest of us were conscious of participating in
historical events of overawing importance. Thousands of veterans must remember our entry into Rome in June 1944, after
the dreary, lethal, and endless winter on the Anzio beachhead
or the Cassino front. Suddenly and as if by magic we were in a
beautiful city, full of sunshine and of excited people intent on
showering us with favors. In place of the sad and dumpy
creatures we had supposed all Italians were, here were fresh-
faced, bare-legged, wonderful girls, hungry for men, who
seemed to regard us when we first entered the city as akin to
demigods. There was something primitive and archaic about
the emotions that swept over all of us on that first glorious day
in Rome. The Eternal City was welcoming another conqueror,
and, as we were hugged and embraced for hours by the ex-

uberant populace, I felt like one of the soldiers who took the city thousands of years before.

And the capture of Rome was nothing more than the most massive of these welcomings. In France it happened in many a town and city that we felt like conquering heroes, that delicious, boyish sense of triumph and elation, ridiculous but irresistible. In my journal I find a brief account of one such occasion, which could stand for many.

My heart is full tonight. We are at Vienne, near Lyons, and were the first Americans in the town. Our reception was unequaled, even by Rome. Everybody was out on the streets, even though it was raining, and we were kissed and showered with flowers for hours. We took the flowers to the grave of the unknown soldier after awhile and then we were really mobbed. Surely no emperor has ever received more sincere and enthusiastic welcome than we. They took us to the famous Point restaurant, and we ate as I have never eaten before in Europe or elsewhere. Then to hotel rooms where each has a room to himself and wonderful beds. Tonight the others have gone on, and I got the owner of the hotel to show me the churches and the town. My first pure Gothic cathedral, 11th century, a refreshment to the spirit like nothing else; then a view of the town from the heights, beautiful under the evening sky, with its red roofs, its Roman remains on adjacent hills. Then later I arranged a coffee-drinking party with the lady in charge of the hotel—an Italian by birth. We had fifteen or twenty men and women there and how they enjoyed the coffee and cigarettes! We are almost like gods to these people. I laugh at myself but I get excited too.

How characteristic that last line is of many moods in those days. One laughed joyously and felt a bit sheepish at the same time. At some level we knew that we were far from being what these people thought us, but it was unbelievably pleasant, nevertheless. It was compensation for the opposite situation

11

and mood, which were our usual lot, for everyone knows that war can be the most excruciatingly boring of all human activities. The alternation of dullness and excitement in their extreme degrees separates war from peace sharply and promotes the discontinuity in our memories. War compresses the greatest opposites into the smallest space and the shortest time.

Not only do boredom and throbbing excitement succeed each other rapidly, but other emotions as well. In a town near Vienne the people divided their attention between cheering us and persecuting collaborators who were being rounded up by the Resistance youth. In the delirium of liberation, many individuals were constantly going from a group that was hugging and kissing returned FFI comrades to join another that was torturing isolated collaborators. We could observe love and hatred, tenderness and brutality, succeed each other in many a person within moments. Excitement was at fever pitch. German soldiers with hands high in the air were being marched to a prisoner collection point by triumphant boys. With a sense of horror, a comrade and I walking the streets watched a group beating a girl whose hair had been crudely sheared off and her face bloodied and bruised. She was crying bitterly as her tormentors kicked her along, taunting and jeering and hooting; evidently she had been the mistress of some German and possibly had spied on the local Resistance. A little further on we saw a man, with his face cut, running like a hurt and frightened beast before men who were doing worse things to him than were happening to the girl. It was clear that he had no chance of remaining alive if and when his pursuers cornered him.

Suddenly from a group perhaps twenty yards ahead of us a girl detached herself and ran directly toward me. Slim and fleet as a deer, she was in my startled arms before I knew what was happening. A hug, a quick kiss on the mouth, and she spun away with flaming cheeks into another crowd in scarcely the time it takes to draw a breath. Everybody laughed happily and applauded, while I picked up my fallen cap and tried to conceal my red face and inner confusion. The act was purely spontaneous; doubtless, in her excitement she hardly knew what she was doing. Nothing could be more typical of the confused emotions of war than that town in the first few hours of freedom from German occupation.

There were other kinds of excitement, not so gleeful, in which the nervous tension was, if possible, even greater. Perhaps no soldier could describe adequately his feelings on a D-day landing under fire. Moods of fear, anticipation, helplessness, praying and cursing, adventure and longing succeed each other like lightning. Though the landing in southern France was a comparatively easy one, its details emerge clearly when I choose to remember them. I crouched under my jeep on a landing craft that went in a few hours after the first waves of infantry. Shells were exploding in the water all around, and I felt sure the next one would land squarely on us. It was silly to expect the jeep to afford any protection against the German 88s, but I could not get up. Then through the tangle of gear and machines I saw an American officer, a captain, standing by the edge of our boat. He was smoking a cigarette, and I watched fascinated as he flicked the ashes into the water. His hand trembled not at all; he might have been on the Staten Island ferry. Then I felt unreasonably grateful to him. It was clear that he was exposing himself no more nor less than I; but his reason was in control. I longed to creep through the gear, clasp him around the knees, and look up to him worshipfully. Yet the ridiculousness of such an action did not chain me so much as the fancied danger of moving from my spot.

Nevertheless, the sight of him gradually calmed me, so that when our craft reached the shore I was able to get into my jeep and drive it hurriedly through the surf and up onto dry land.

In a grove a few hundred yards inland, we had to stop and peel the protective putty from our motors, which had kept them from drowning out in the shallow water. Again the shells began to discover our location and to get close. Finally one plopped among us, and as I threw myself down I waited for the fragments to dig into my flesh. All that hit me was dirt and little stones thrown up by the shell. But it scared me unreasonably; the next one, I was sure, would be the end for me. I had no cover, so I got up and ran for the nearest protection I could find, which was very inadequate. There I discovered other soldiers as near to Mother Nature as they could get. I followed their example and began digging a slit trench among the rocks with my fingernails. The next explosion was farther off, and we began to breathe easier. After a while we went back, and discovered that the jeep next to mine had huge holes through the engine. Other nearby vehicles were in similar condition.

Such external descriptions give little idea of the racing excitement that underlies the occasion. And landings are only an outstanding instance. Anyone who has lived through an air raid of any magnitude at all knew a quality of excitement scarcely experienced before or since. Fear may have been the dominant feature of such excitement; rarely was it the only ingredient. In such an emotional situation there is often a surge of vitality and a glimpse of potentialities, of what we really are or have been or might become, as fleeting as it is genuine. In these situations some are able to serve others in simple yet fundamental ways. Inhuman cruelty can give way to superhuman kindness. Inhibitions vanish, and people are reduced to their essence. If afterward they seem quickly to forget, perhaps the memory is not wholly lost. Again and again in moments of this kind I was as much inspired by the nobility of some of my fellows as appalled by the animality of others, or, more exactly, by both qualities in the same person. The average degree, which we commonly know in peacetime, conceals as much as it reveals about the human creature.

Then there was the strange. I think every soldier must have felt at times that this or that happening fitted into nothing that had gone before; it was incomprehensible, either absurd or mysterious or both. If many events of this sort came to us, we began to feel foreign to our own skins, intruders in the world. More often than at home, we would wake up in the night and wonder where we were. And, our senses fully recovered in a few seconds, we might begin to ponder what it meant to be where we were. I suppose this feeling of strangeness came over us so often because of our comrades. Since they were not chosen and usually had no prewar connection with each other or each other's home towns, however dear they had become in military life, they represented discontinuity with all but the present and the immediate past.

I confess that a large number of Americans I met in the Army amazed me by their differentness. I had not known their like before, nor have I met them since. Nothing else could have made me realize how narrow the circle in which we move in peacetime is. Most of us hardly get an inkling of how ninety per cent of our fellows live or think. Naïvely we assume that they must be like us or not very different.

Whatever the cause, I was surely not alone in being under the spell of the strange. Sometimes I moved through days and weeks trying to reach the familiar, the accustomed, and the intimate. Through the study of Hegel in college and graduate school, I had adopted the life goal of becoming at home in the world. Now it became remote to the vanishing point, for I could not banish the alien character of much of my experience. Again my journal bears witness to the recurring nature of this dominant mood.

November 6, 1944. A curious incident occurred today, which, like the Lorelei tale, will not leave my mind. This morning two FFI [French Forces of the Interior] boys who are working for us came in with a story of having seen a suspicious soldier in the forest who had German weapons and who spoke only French or perhaps German. He was by himself and collected rations which were strewn about the woods. They thought he was possibly a German who had got into American uniform and was hiding out. I decided to go with them this afternoon to investigate.

It was a rainy, dark day. We drove the jeep through a forest trail that had evidently been the scene of a bitter battle. Trees were razed; once we had to remove one from the trail. I was nervous about mines, since the road showed little trace of American vehicular traffic, though the boys kept assuring me that it had been traversed. Finally we could go no farther by jeep and had to proceed by foot. The woods were rain-soaked and dripping and the ground was soggy underfoot. The stillness was impressive and somehow threatening. No sign of life was visible and the evidence of recent battle was everywhere. Deep and elaborate foxholes lined the trail, around which were strewn all manner of equipment, German and American: ammunition, helmets, clothing, letters from home, everything. We finally came upon the body of a German soldier, missed by the collection unit. He was lying in the distorted position common to all who are killed in action. Someone had pulled his coat over his head, and when one of us raised it we saw that he had been shot in the head and was already decomposing. His diary and other papers were lying near, but I did not read them. He seemed to fit in with this dark scene and dark day. I noticed as we continued our tramp that I felt a little sick in my stomach. The macabre aspect of this adventure was like something out of Edgar Allan Poe. Next we came upon a peasant couple digging busily at the remains of an entrenchment, obviously on the search for whatever of value they could find. They looked up a little guiltily when we bore down on them and responded hastily to the question of one of the FFI that they had seen no one.

We continued on our way and at last arrived at a little depression in the woods, formed like a basin. On its floor there was constructed a rude hut from a foxhole, about three feet high and covered over with all manner of materials from logs to uniforms. This was apparently our quarry, for the boys silently deployed around it, guns at the ready. I had forgotten mine, so merely stood by. One of them called out: Hände hoch! *Almost at once there emerged a head from the single opening, and then a tall, unshaven, and unkempt soldier crawled out and stood up. He was in American uniform, and after a moment's hesitation, I asked: "Are you an American?" He answered: "Yes." Then I knew that he was a deserter. I jumped down into the basin and approached him. It was evident that his nerves were bad because he was near to crying.*

He had been there about a week and had made himself fairly comfortable. Inside the hut he had a fire going and had just cooked a meal. At first he lied to me a little about his unit, but when he saw that I was disposed to be kind, he told me all. He had been overseas more than two years and had fought with the ——th in Africa, Sicily, and Italy, then got transferred to the —— for France.

"All the men I knew and trained with have been killed or transferred," he said with a quaver in his voice. "I'm lonely. They promised me I would be relieved and rotated, but nothing ever happens. I can't stand the infantry any longer. Why won't they transfer me to some other outfit? The shells seem to come closer all the time and I can't stand them." He shivered. I let him talk and tried to be as sympathetic as I could. I felt terribly sorry for

17

*him. He was from Pennsylvania, not a bright lad but very literate.
He begged me to let him stay there for a few more days, after
which he promised to rejoin his unit voluntarily. "I'm used to
living out in the woods," he said. "At home I always camped out
a lot." But he did not argue much when I explained that I could
not do it and that a few days later would not help him much. "I'm
glad you took me in and not the Military Police," he said and
offered me his German P-38 pistol, evidently a prized possession.
"The MPs will take it away from me and I'd rather you had it."
I protested but finally suggested that he should give it to me and
I would send it to his home after the war. I took down his mother's
address and shall return it to him someday. He was grateful, particularly when I made the FFI give him his German field glasses,
which he thought the MPs would allow him to keep.*

*We started the long walk back through the dripping woods,
after the FFI boys had gathered up the rations, blankets, and other
equipment. The deserter was certain that they had reported him
in order to get his rations because they had been there before and
tried to take them. He said they were aware that he was an American. After a while I strongly suspected that he was right. I let
them lug the food and keep it but I took the blankets and equipment to the Prisoner of War Cage and turned him and his belongings over to the Military Police. They appeared to receive him
matter-of-factly and I suspect that he will not be punished but
simply put back into the line again, as he bitterly predicted.*

*To ask the question Ernst Jünger asks in his war diary of
1940: Why was I brought before this scene? There may be a
good reason. Despite the seeming arbitrariness of everything, I
still believe that our lives are directed. When I cease to believe
that I shall be ready for death.*

Strangest of all to me, and from present perspective most
significant, was an encounter in Italy a few weeks after we
were committed to the front lines. In a free hour one day I
climbed one of the nearby hills of the Apennines and got off
by myself in the late afternoon sun. Passing through olive

groves, I soon got away from the evidences of war and gradually came near the top of the ridge. There I came upon an old hermit, who was sitting upon the grass of a cleared space, smoking a battered old pipe while his donkey grazed nearby. A sod hut into which I peered contained only a clean pallet of straw and a few simple cooking utensils. The old man greeted me amiably, and we fell into conversation, though communication was not easy owing to his dialect and my imperfect mastery of Italian, which was drawn largely from grammars. He was smoking dried grass, and his grizzled features took on a delighted smile when on my invitation he replaced this with good American tobacco.

Down in the valley the evening cannonade began, and in the distance we could see where the shells from both sides originated and, a few seconds later, where some of them landed with huge dust clouds and explosions. The hermit began to gesticulate and to question me, and it gradually became clear to me that he was mystified by all this and wanted an explanation of what was going on. Could it be, I asked myself, that he does not know about the war? And there flashed into my mind a remark of Tolstoi's in *War and Peace* to the effect that many Russian peasants who suffered loss of everything in Napoleon's invasion of Russia had not the faintest idea from first to last who was making war or what the campaigns were about. That, however, was in a novel. Here, more than a century later, I had stumbled on a man who was totally detached from what was absorbing my whole life and the lives of millions like me.

Perplexed, I tried to explain simply in my halting Italian what World War II was all about. Then it gradually dawned on me how impossible my task really was and would be even though I spoke a perfect dialect Italian. How could one explain to this illiterate old man why Americans and British and Germans, with some of his countrymen on both sides, were fighting in Italy? Did I myself know in other than a superficial sense? The strangeness of the conflict and my part in it made me shiver. Why were we fighting individuals whom we had never seen and who had never seen us, soldiers who were probably as miserable and ignorant as we? What was I doing here? How did this mad war concern me? For a few minutes I could observe this spectacle through the puzzled eyes of the old hermit, long enough to realize that I understood it as little as he.

It is hard to put into words the conflicting ideas that raced through my mind as I said good-by to the innocent old man and started down the ridge. I felt keenly what the philosopher Karl Jaspers calls the bottomlessness of the world. The professors who had taught me philosophy and for whom I had had great respect and esteem became all at once puny in my imagination. I pictured them at this moment sitting around their radios at home listening for news of what we were doing here and understanding it as little as the hermit and I. Even the great thinkers of Western civilization seemed suddenly to lose their stature and become only human beings, unable to help me fathom what millions of Europeans and Asians were undergoing at this moment. Their wisdom was almost grotesquely inadequate for the occasion. I knew then that I could rely no longer on them for help; there was no one but myself.

If there was a dominant mood in my whirling thoughts, it was one of exposure, resulting from my loss of hold on tradition and the protection of nature now torn by conflict. I was amazed at my former simple-mindedness and glad, despite everything, to be finally aware of it. There was a rare element of liberation about this experience of strangeness, not present in the others. I realized my powerlessness to escape further involvement in the war, mad and meaningless though it might be. But by the time I had reached my quarters, I had achieved a degree of detachment, through heightened self-awareness, impossible to those unfortunate men who gained no respite from battle. I was not again to enter the conflict as a victim in quite the same way as before. Inwardly I was shielded from the danger of false hopes and faith in the outcome of the war, to some extent, also, from false loves and hates.

In some sense I had come to myself, as is reported of the prodigal son, and this meant that some simple and familiar things were seen for the first time in a proper light. In our normal state we seem to be remote from the plainest and most important truths. "It is quite in keeping with man's curious intellectual history," writes Norman Angell, "that the simplest and most important questions are those he asks least often." Perhaps the reason is that the required naïveté is not easy to acquire or retain. The insights of one hour are blotted out by the events of the next, and few of us can hold on to our real selves long enough to discover the momentous truths about ourselves and this whirling earth to which we cling. This is especially true of men at war. The great god Mars tries to blind us when we enter his realm, and when we leave he gives us a generous cup of the waters of Lethe to drink.

Though I did not forget my encounter with the hermit, the necessities of action took hold of me once more. When the war finally ended for me, in the heart of Germany sixteen crowded months later, the cruel, the momentous, and the strange were blended as never before. Emotionally I had grown numb, so I thought, but to my surprise I discovered on V-E Day that I could not keep tears from my eyes. Most of all, I was pained at the thought of those who had lost their lives in the last few days of fighting. How could I ever make sense of the tragedy of those, in concentration camp and front line, who had longed for this day through the years only to perish a few hours or days before its dawn? Why had I been spared? To these questions no answer came.

The next months were a severe struggle with restlessness, a nearly universal disease of that period and not at all confined to veteran soldiers. At times I wanted to transfer to UNRRA and help rebuild the shattered countries I had done my bit to tear down. At other times I wanted to escape the charnel house of Europe and seek to find myself in the profession I had prepared for in years that now appeared incredibly remote. When a job offer unexpectedly came from an American college president, I did not know whether I was glad or sorry. It set me dreaming of teaching sober, interested students, working out with them some of the tormenting problems of life and thought. But could I endure big, blustering, unrepentant America? I speculated in my journal on what I would answer if the college president were to ask me what my philosophic position was, and decided I would answer that I was a brokenhearted idealist, realizing that, while such an answer would not stand for much in formal philosophy, it had a significance for me that he could scarcely fathom.

However, the passage of time puts a new face on everything. I soon got out of the Army and gradually I got used to peacetime ways again. It seems scarcely credible to me now that for a period I felt curiously undressed without a pistol on my hip, and I trod softly for a while on all loose sod, unconsciously fearing booby traps, those devilish antipersonnel mines designed to kill or castrate the unwary soldier who stepped on one. When a new generation of college students replaced the veterans with whom I could philosophize meaningfully without mentioning our common past, the war receded even faster than before. Now it is almost as though it never took place.

Yet something is wrong, dreadfully wrong. When I consider how easily we forget the millions who suffered unbearably, either permanently maimed in body or mind, or who gave up their lives before they had realized their purposes, I rebel at the whole insane spectacle of human existence. Had I been one of them, how little difference it would make to anyone today. Are we, the survivors, changed at all in significant ways as a consequence of World War II? Am I? And if so, how?

Answering for myself only, I must say: Not nearly enough. Despite the mood of my letter from Alsace, I have not adopted the Christian injunction or heeded Auden's warning. Instead, I have yielded to an old temptation. So often in the war I felt an utter dissociation from what had gone before in my life; since then I have experienced an absence of continuity between those years and what I have become. As a teacher of philosophy and would-be philosopher, I strive to see at least my own life as a whole and to discover some purpose and direction in at least the major parts. Yet the effort to assimilate those intense war memories to the rest of my experience is difficult and even frightening. Why attempt it? Why not continue to forget?

It is a real temptation, urged upon us by many. There is a popular belief that the men who knew war at firsthand talk little or not at all about it. Those who do are suspected of wanting to magnify their little egos, of being professional legionnaires. Besides, people are tired of war; one can hear the refrain in a thousand living rooms. They want to read about it as fiction, and so transmute war into art, or have it as history, in memoirs of generals and statesmen. These, admirable as the good ones are, do not make heavy demands on us to assimilate, to bridge the abyss between peace and war. They rarely ask why and to what purpose, and are strangely incurious concerning the psychological and moral interrelations of man as warrior and as civilian.

I am afraid to forget. I fear that we human creatures do not forget cleanly, as the animals presumably do. What protrudes and does not fit in our pasts rises to haunt us and make us spiritually unwell in the present. The discontinuities in contemporary life are cutting us off from our roots and threatening us with the dread evil of nihilism in the twentieth century. We may become refugees in an inner sense unless we remember to some purpose. Surely the menace of new and more frightful wars is not entirely unrelated to our failure to understand those recently fought. If we could gain only a modicum of greater wisdom concerning what manner of men we are, what effect might it not have on future events?

It is exceedingly unlikely that I shall ever be able to understand the why and wherefore of war. But sufficient reflection through the mirror of memory may enable me to make sense of my own small career. The deepest fear of my war years, one still with me, is that these happenings had no real purpose. Just as chance often appeared to rule my course then, so the more ordered paths of peace might well signify nothing or nothing much. This conclusion I am unwilling to accept without a struggle; indeed, I cannot accept it at all except as a counsel of despair. How often I wrote in my war journals that unless that day had some positive significance for my future life, it could not possibly be worth the pain it cost.

TWO

THE
ENDURING
APPEALS
OF BATTLE

I feel cheerful and am well-pleased. . . . . What is ahead may be grim and dreadful but I shall be spiritually more at rest in the heart of the carnage than somewhere in the rear. Since I have lent myself to the war, I want to pay the price and know it at its worst. (War journal, January 31, 1944)

My friend wrote once late in the war that he often thought of me as *the soldier*. To him I had come to stand for the qualities that he associated with universal man at war. The idea, I recall, both flattered and insulted me a little at first but ended by impressing me with its truth, though I should never have conceived it on my own. I wrote in my journal: "Perhaps the worst that can be said is that I am *becoming* a soldier. To be a soldier! That is at best to be something less

than a man. To say nothing of being a philosopher." Since
then I have frequently wondered what it meant to be a
"soldier" and why I regarded myself then, insofar as I was a
soldier, as less than a man.

At the time I wrote these lines I faced the grim realization
of how narrowed all our desires had become. The night before,
one of the women in the town where we were staying had
declared: *"Das Essen ist die Hauptsache."* Food is the main
thing. And the words had burned into my brain with the force
of a proverb. The majority of my fellows seemed content with
the satisfaction of their natural urges—eating, drinking, and
lusting for women. Interests and refinements that transcended
these primitive needs, and that I had built up over the years,
were rapidly falling away, and I felt that I was becoming
simply one of the others.

In a German newspaper, taken from a prisoner, I read a
letter from a soldier long years on the Russian front, who
lamented that the war had robbed him of any sense of self-
identity and that he no longer possessed an ego and a personal
fate. I realize now, much better than I did then, that there was
another force much more determining than simple need and
desire. It was the emotional environment of warfare, more
specifically, the atmosphere of violence. The threat to life and
safety that the presence of the opponent, "the enemy," represented created this climate of feeling. Near the front it was
impossible to ignore, consciously or unconsciously, the stark
fact that out there were men who would gladly kill you, if and
when they got the chance. As a consequence, an individual was
dependent on others, on people who could not formerly have
entered the periphery of his consciousness. For them in turn,
he was of interest only as a center of force, a wielder of

weapons, a means of security and survival. This confraternity of danger and exposure is unequaled in forging links among people of unlike desire and temperament, links that are utilitarian and narrow but no less passionate because of their accidental and general character.

In such a climate men may hold fast in memory to their civilian existence of yesterday and stubbornly resist, as I tried to do, the encroachments of the violent and the irrational. They may write home to their parents and sweethearts that they are unchanged, and they may even be convinced of it. But the soldier who has yielded himself to the fortunes of war, has sought to kill and to escape being killed, or who has even lived long enough in the disordered landscape of battle, is no longer what he was. He becomes in some sense a fighter, whether he wills it or not—at least most men do. His moods and disposition are affected by the presence of others and the encompassing environment of threat and fear. He must surrender in a measure to the will of others and to superior force. In a real sense he becomes a fighting man, a *Homo furens*.

This is surely part of what it means to be a soldier, and what it has always meant. *Homo furens* is, so to speak, a subspecies of the genus Homo sapiens. Obviously, man is more than a fighter and other than a fighter, in our age and formerly. In some generations—alas! too few as yet—organized war has been little more than an episode. Even those generations who have had to spend much time in combat considered themselves farmers, teachers, factory workers, and so on, as well as fighters. Man as warrior is only partly a man, yet, fatefully enough, this aspect of him is capable of transforming the whole. When given free play, it is able to subordinate other aspects of the personality, repress civilian

27

habits of mind, and make the soldier as fighter a different kind of creature from the former worker, farmer, or clerk.

Millions of men in our day—like millions before us—have learned to live in war's strange element and have discovered in it a powerful fascination. The emotional environment of warfare has always been compelling; it has drawn most men under its spell. Reflection and calm reasoning are alien to it. I wrote in my war journal that I was obsessed with "the tyranny of the present"; the past and the future did not concern me. It was hard for me to think, to be alone. When the signs of peace were visible, I wrote, in some regret: "The purgative force of danger which makes men coarser but perhaps more human will soon be lost and the first months of peace will make some of us yearn for the old days of conflict."

Beyond doubt there are many who simply endure war, hating every moment. Though they may enjoy garrison life or military maneuvers, they experience nothing but distaste and horror for combat itself. Still, those who complain the most may not be immune from war's appeals. Soldiers complain as an inherited right and traditional duty, and few wish to admit to a taste for war. Yet many men both hate and love combat. They know why they hate it; it is harder to know and to be articulate about why they love it. The novice may be eager at times to describe his emotions in combat, but it is the battle-hardened veterans to whom battle has offered the deeper appeals. For some of them the war years are what Dixon Wecter has well called "the one great lyric passage in their lives."

What are these secret attractions of war, the ones that have persisted in the West despite revolutionary changes in the methods of warfare? I believe that they are: the delight in seeing, the delight in comradeship, the delight in destruction. Some fighters know one appeal and not the others, some experience all three, and some may, of course, feel other appeals that I do not know. These three had reality for me, and I have found them also throughout the literature of war.

War as a spectacle, as something to see, ought never to be underestimated. There is in all of us what the Bible calls "the lust of the eye," a phrase at once precise and of the widest connotation. It is precise because human beings possess as a primitive urge this love of watching. We fear we will miss something worth seeing. This passion to see surely precedes in most of us the urge to participate in or to aid. Anyone who has watched people crowding around the scene of an accident on the highway realizes that the lust of the eye is real. Anyone who has watched the faces of people at a fire knows it is real. Seeing sometimes absorbs us utterly; it is as though the human being became one great eye. The eye is lustful because it requires the novel, the unusual, the spectacular. It cannot satiate itself on the familiar, the routine, the everyday.

This lust may stoop to mindless curiosity, a primordial impulse. Its typical response is an open-minded gaping at a parade or at the explosion of a hydrogen bomb. How many men in each generation have been drawn into the twilight of confused and murderous battle "to see what it is like"? This appeal of war is usually described as the desire to escape the monotony of civilian life and the cramping restrictions of an unadventurous existence. People are often bored with a day that does not offer variety, distraction, threat, and insecurity. They crave the satisfaction of the astonishing. Although war notoriously offers monotony and boredom enough, it also offers the outlandish, the exotic, and the strange. It offers the opportunity of gaping at other lands and other peoples, at curious implements of war, at groups of others like themselves marching in order, and at the captured enemy in a cage.

However, sensuous curiosity is only one level of seeing. The word "see," with its many derivatives, like "insight" and "vision," has an imaginative and intellectual connotation which is far more expansive than the physical. Frequently we are unable to separate these levels of seeing, to distinguish the outer from the inner eye. This is probably no accident. The human being is, after all, a unity, and the sensuous, imaginative, and intellectual elements of his nature can fuse when he is absorbed. Mindless curiosity is not separated as much as we like to believe from what art lovers call the disinterested contemplation of beauty. The delight in battle as a mere spectacle may progress almost insensibly to an aesthetic contemplation or to a more dominantly intellectual contemplation of its awfulness. From the simplest soldier who gazes openmouthed at the panorama of battle in his portion of the field to the trained artist observing the scene, there is, I believe, only a difference of degree. The "seeing" both are engaged in is for them an end in itself before it becomes a spur to action. The dominant motive in both cases appears to be neither the desire for knowledge, though there is much that is instructive in the scene, nor the need to act, though that, too, will become imperative. Their "seeing" is for the sake of seeing, the lust of the eye, where the eye stands for the whole human being, for man the observer.

There is a popular conviction that war and battle are the sphere of ugliness, and, since aesthetic delight is associated with the beautiful, it may be concluded that war is the natural enemy of the aesthetic. I fear that this is in large part an illusion. It is, first of all, wrong to believe that only beauty can give us aesthetic delight; the ugly can please us too, as every artist knows. And furthermore, beauty in various guises is hardly foreign to scenes of battle. While it is undeniable that the disorder and distortion and the violation of nature that conflict brings are ugly beyond compare, there are also color and movement, variety, panoramic sweep, and sometimes even momentary proportion and harmony. If we think of beauty and ugliness without their usual moral overtones, there is often a weird but genuine beauty in the sight of massed men and weapons in combat. Reputedly, it was the sight of advancing columns of men under fire that impelled General Robert E. Lee to remark to one of his staff: "It is well that war is so terrible—we would grow too fond of it."

Of course, it is said that modern battles lack all the color and magnificence of spectacle common to earlier wars. John Neff, in his valuable study entitled *War and Human Progress*, makes much of the decline in our century of the power and authority of what he calls "the claims of delight." In earlier times men at war, he points out, were much more dominated by artistic considerations in the construction of their weapons. They insisted on the decorative and beautiful in cannons, ships, and small arms, even at the obvious expense of the practical and militarily effective. Then, artists of great skill and fame worked on weapons of war, and gunsmiths took great pride in the beauty of their products. The claims of beauty, Neff believes, have had to give way more and more to materialistic and pragmatic aims in this century of total warfare. When I remember some of the hideous implements of battle in World War II, it is hard indeed not to agree with him. Standardization and automatization of weapons have frequently stripped them of any pretense to beauty.

This, though, is only one aspect of battle and of modern war. What has been lost in one realm is compensated for in

31

another. War is now fought in the air as well as on land and sea, and the expanse of vision and spectacle afforded by combat planes is hard to exaggerate. Because these powerful new weapons usually remove those who use them further from the gruesome consequences of their firing, they afford more opportunity for aesthetic satisfaction. Combat in the skies is seldom devoid of the form, grace, and harmony that ground fighting lacks. There are spectacular sweep and drama, a colorfulness and a precision about such combat which earlier centuries knew only in a few great sea battles. It is true that the roar of fighting planes can be unpleasant in its assault upon the ears, and their dives upon their victims for strafing or bombing can be terror-inspiring. But the combatant who is relieved from participation and given the spectator's role can nearly sate the eye with all the elements of fearful beauty.

I remember most vividly my feelings while watching from a landing boat, on the morning of August 25, 1944, the simultaneous bombardment of the French Riviera by our planes and by our fleet of warships. We had come relatively close to the targets under the cover of darkness. As dawn broke and the outline of the coast appeared, thousands of us watched motionless and silent, conscious that we would be called upon to act only after the barrage and bombing were over. Then we saw the planes, appearing from nowhere, and in perfect alignment over their targets. Suddenly, fire and smoke issued from huge cannon on our ships, and the invasion had begun. Our eyes followed the planes as they dived into the melee of smoke and flame and dust and emerged farther down the coast to circle for another run. The assault of bomb and shell on the line of coast was so furious that I half expected a large part of the mainland to become somehow detached and fall into the sea.

When I could forget the havoc and terror that was being created by those shells and bombs among the half-awake inhabitants of the villages, the scene was beyond all question magnificent. I found it easily possible, indeed a temptation hard to resist, to gaze upon the scene spellbound, completely absorbed, indifferent to what the immediate future might bring. Others appeared to manifest a similar intense concentration on the spectacle. Many former soldiers must be able to recall some similar experience. However incomprehensible such scenes may be, and however little anyone would want to see them enacted a second time, few of us can deny, if we are honest, a satisfaction in having seen them. As far as I am concerned, at least part of that satisfaction can be ascribed to delight in aesthetic contemplation.

As I reflect further, it becomes clear, however, that the term "beauty," used in any ordinary sense, is not the major appeal in such spectacles. Instead, it is the fascination that manifestations of power and magnitude hold for the human spirit. Some scenes of battle, much like storms over the ocean or sunsets on the desert or the night sky seen through a telescope, are able to overawe the single individual and hold him in a spell. He is lost in their majesty. His ego temporarily deserts him, and he is absorbed into what he sees. An awareness of power that far surpasses his limited imagination transports him into a state of mind unknown in his everyday experiences. Fleeting as these rapt moments may be, they are, for the majority of men, an escape from themselves that is very different from the escapes induced by sexual love or alcohol. This raptness is a joining and not a losing, a deprivation of self in exchange for a union with objects that were hitherto foreign. Yes, the chief aesthetic appeal of war surely lies in this feeling of the sublime, to which we, children of nature, are directed whether we desire it or not. Astonishment and wonder and awe appear to be part of our deepest being, and war offers them an exercise field par excellence. As I wrote:

Yesterday morning we left Rome and took up the pursuit of the rapidly fleeing Germans. And again the march was past ruined, blackened villages, destroyed vehicles, dead and mangled corpses of German soldiers, dead and stinking horses, blown bridges, and clouds of dust that blackened our faces and filled our clothes. . . . Later I watched a full moon sail through a cloudy sky . . . saw German bombers fly past and our antiaircraft bursts around them. . . . I felt again the aching beauty of this incomparable land. I remembered everything that I had ever been and was. It was painful and glorious.

What takes place in us when we are under the spell of this powerful mood? It is often said that its deepest satisfaction lies in the sense of personal exemption from the fate of others. We watch them exposed to powers that overwhelm them, and we enjoy the feelings of superiority of the secure. When human beings are not involved, and feelings of the sublime steal over us at the majestic in nature, this can be traced to a heightened sense of the ego in one way or another. As spectators we are superior to that which we survey. In my journal are these words:

This evening we watched a beautiful sunset over the Tyrrhenian Sea. From our window we looked out on the wall-enclosed gardens of Carano, where flowers blossomed and peach trees made the air sweet with their white blossoms. Beyond them stretched fields and, farther, the mountains, Formia, Gaeta, the sea. As the sun sank behind the mountains, it illumined a cloud that was hanging low. As we watched the wonderful pageantry of nature, the sound of cannon was carried in on the evening air. We were forced to realize that a few miles away, in this area we were gazing at, men lurked with death in their hearts. We were looking over no man's

*land. As it grew dark, huge signs of fire appeared on the moun-
tain. It was mysterious, but we had no doubt that it had to do
with death and destruction.*

The feeling of momentary depression, as Kant puts it, which
we initially succumb to when looking through a telescope
at the vastness of the heavens and the insignificance of ourselves in comparison is soon supplanted by the consciousness that we are the astronomers. It is we who know that the
heavens are empty and vast, and the heavens presumably
know nothing of us. The human spirit triumphs over these
blind forces and lifeless powers of nature. Such scenes as I
described above could be explained, by this view, as the exultation of the spectators that they were not actors or sufferers,
for the sublime mood derives from a separation of the spectator from the spectacle, and its pleasantness consists in the
superiority the ego feels.

But such a view is wrong, or, at the very least, one-sided.
It is the viewpoint of an egoistic, atomistic psychology rather
than the product of close observation. The awe that steals over
us at such times is not essentially a feeling of triumph, but,
on the contrary, a recognition of power and grandeur to which
we are subject. There is not so much a separation of the self
from the world as a subordination of the self to it. We are
able to disregard personal danger at such moments by transcending the self, by forgetting our separateness.

*Last evening I sat on a rock outside the town and watched a
modern battle, an artillery duel . . . the panorama was so far-
reaching that I could see both the explosion of the guns and
where their speedy messengers struck. . . . Several shells of reply-
ing batteries landed fairly close and made my perch not the safest
of vantage points. But it was an interesting, stirring sight. After a
while the firing died down and evening shadows came over the*

valley. A townsman carrying a pail of swill for his hogs came by, fell into conversation, and then asked me to await his return, when he would take me to his home for a glass of wine.

Perhaps the majority of men cannot become so absorbed in a spectacle that they overcome fear of pain and death. Still, it is a common-enough phenomenon on the battlefield that men expose themselves quite recklessly for the sake of seeing. If ever the world is blown to bits by some superbomb, there will be those who will watch the spectacle to the last minute, without fear, disinterestedly and with detachment. I do not mean that there is lack of interest in this disinterestedness or lack of emotion in this detachment. Quite the contrary. But the self is no longer important to the observer; it is absorbed into the objects with which it is concerned.

I think the distinctive thing about the feeling of the sublime is its ecstatic character, ecstatic in the original meaning of the term, namely, a state of being outside the self. Even in the common experience of mindless curiosity there is a momentary suppression of the ego, a slight breaking down of the barriers of the self, though insignificant in comparison with the rarer moods when we are filled with awe. This ecstasy satisfies because we are conscious of a power outside us with which we can merge in the relation of parts to whole. Feelings neither of triumph nor of depression predominate. The pervasive sense of wonder satisfies us because we are assured that we are part of this circling world, not divorced from it, or shut up within the walls of the self and delivered over to the insufficiency of the ego. Certain psychologists would call this just another escape from the unpleasant facts of the self's situation. If so, it is an escape of a very different sort from the usual. We feel rescued from the emptiness within us. In losing ourselves we gain a relationship to something greater than the self, and the foreign character of the surrounding world is drastically reduced.

A good example of what I am saying can be found in a little book entitled *Letzte Briefe aus Stalingrad* (Last Letters from Stalingrad). In 1943 the German high command, anxious to assess the morale of the encircled soldiers at Stalingrad, sent word that mail would be forwarded to their homes by plane. Since the situation had become desperate, most of the men understood that this would probably be their last communication with home. After the letters were written, they were requisitioned by German security officers and never delivered to the addressees. At the end of the war, the packets of letters were discovered in police buildings, and a selection from them, without the names of the men who wrote them, was published in Germany. These letters, intended only for the eyes of loved ones by men who were experiencing the bitter shock of military defeat after spectacular victories, have a stark quality seldom found in war literature. The following translation is from the first one in the little volume, and is obviously from the hand of a military meteorologist:

My life has not changed at all. Just as it was ten years ago, my life is blessed by the stars and shunned by man. I had even then no friends and you know why they avoided me. My happiness was to sit in front of the telescope and peer at the sky and the world of the stars, pleased as a child who is allowed to play with the stars.

You were my best friend, Monika. No, you read it aright; you were my best friend. The time is too serious for joking. This letter will need fourteen days to reach you. By that time you will have read in the papers what has happened here. Don't think too much about it. The facts will be quite different from what you read, but let other people worry about setting them straight. I have always thought in light-years and felt in seconds. Here too

I am busy with recording weather conditions. Four of us are working together and if things would go on like this, we would be content. The work itself is easy. We have the task of recording temperature and humidity, reporting on cloudiness and visibility. If one of these bureaucrats were to read what I am writing, his eyes would pop—violation of security!

Monika, what does our life amount to in comparison with the millions of years of the starry heavens! Andromeda and Pegasus are just over my head on this lovely night. I have been looking at them for a long time; soon I shall be near them. I can thank the stars for my contentment and serenity. You are, of course, for me the most beautiful star! The stars are immortal and the life of man is like a particle of dust in the universe.

Everything around us is collapsing, a whole army is dying, and night and day are aflame. And four people are busily recording temperatures and cloud conditions! I don't understand much about war. No human being has ever fallen by my hand. I never even aimed my pistol at a target. But this I do know: our opponents do not demonstrate our lack of intelligence. I would have liked to continue counting stars for a few decades but nothing will come of it now.

This letter, from a German soldier, reveals, I think, the writer's power to attach himself to the things of nature and feel their kinship to him even in a world aflame. At moments he does feel his moral responsibility to a human being who probably loves him and will mourn for him. "You are, of course, for me the most beautiful star!" The "of course" sounds like a twinge of conscience which reveals where his real heart lies, for his thoughts whirl immediately back again to his vision of the truly important and immortal things of the universe, which he hopes soon to be approaching. Even in a situation where safety and life itself are at stake, this soldier holds fast to his feelings of kinship with the universe about him and loses himself in contemplating its wonders. To be sure, he is doubtless an exception. He tells us himself that he was accustomed to being alone with his thoughts a great deal, and he is an astronomer. Perhaps most soldiers are incapable of carrying absorption so far. Yet many have felt similar urgings toward the infinite in moments of extremity, and, though they cannot be articulate about such experiences, they are rarely quite the same afterward.

If the delight in seeing, especially in its higher reaches, appears to be a noble quality in men, we should not forget one salient fact: It nearly always involves a neglect of moral ideals and an absence of concern for the practical. That is why the lust of the eye is roundly condemned in Biblical context. Morality involves action, while seeing, in all of its meanings, is a fugitive from action. Morality is based on the social; the ecstatic, on the other hand, is transsocial. The fulfillment of the aesthetic is in contemplation, and it shuns the patience and the hard work that genuine morality demands. The deterioration of moral fervor, which is a consequence of every war, may not be entirely due to the reversal of values that fighting and killing occasion. May it not be also a consequence of aesthetic ecstasy, which is always pressing us beyond the border of the morally permissible? The experience in memory may be uncanny and leave no desire for repetition. Yet we find it difficult after the war to regain the full conviction of previous moral goals.

Another appeal of war, the communal experience we call comradeship, is thought, on the other hand, to be especially moral and the one genuine advantage of battle that peace can seldom offer. Whether this is true or not deserves to be investigated. The term "comradeship" covers a large number of relationships, from the most personal to the anonymous and

39

general, and here I will consider only some essentials of military comradeship. What calls it into being in battle, what strengthens or weakens it, what is its essential attraction?

The feeling of belonging together that men in battle often find a cementing force needs first to be awakened by an external reason for fighting, but the feeling is by no means dependent on this reason. The cause that calls comradeship into being may be the defense of one's country, the propagation of the one true religious faith, or a passionate political ideology; it may be the maintenance of honor or the recovery of a Helen of Troy. So long as there is a cause, the hoped-for objective may be relatively unimportant in itself. When, through military reverses or the fatiguing and often horrible experiences of combat, the original purpose becomes obscured, the fighter is often sustained solely by the determination not to let down his comrades.

Numberless soldiers have died, more or less willingly, not for country or honor or religious faith or for any other abstract good, but because they realized that by fleeing their post and rescuing themselves, they would expose their companions to greater danger. Such loyalty to the group is the essence of fighting morale. The commander who can preserve and strengthen it knows that all other psychological or physical factors are little in comparison. The feeling of loyalty, it is clear, is the result, and not the cause, of comradeship. Comrades are loyal to each other spontaneously and without any need for reasons. Men may learn to be loyal out of fear or from rational conviction, loyal even to those they dislike. But such loyalty is rarely reliable with great masses of men unless it has some cement in spontaneous liking and the feeling of belonging.

Though comradeship is dependent on being together physically in time and space, it is not a herding animal instinct. Little can be learned, I am convinced, from attempting to compare animal and human forms of association. In extreme danger and need, there is undeniably a minimal satisfaction in having others of your own species in your vicinity. The proverb that "misery loves company" is not without basis, particularly in situations where defense and aggression are involved. But it is equally true that men can live in the same room and share the same suffering without any sense of belonging together. They can live past each other and be irresponsible toward each other, even when their welfare is clearly dependent on co-operation.

German soldiers who endured Russian prisoner-of-war camps in the decade after World War II have described convincingly how the Communist system succeeded in destroying any sense of comradeship among prisoners simply by making the results of individual labor the basis of food allotments. Under a system like this, men can not only eat their fill but also enjoy superfluity without any concern for a mate who may slowly be starving to death. This lamentable fact about human nature has too often been observed to require much further confirmation. The physical proximity of men can do no more than create the minimal conditions of comradeship. It no more explains the communal appeal of war than it explains why people love cities.

What then are the important components of comradeship, if physical presence is only a minimal condition? The one that occurs immediately is organization for a common goal. Even a very loose type of organization can induce many people to moderate their self-assertiveness and accommodate themselves to the direction of a superpersonal will. Everyone is aware of the vast difference between a number of men as a chance collection of individuals and the same number as an organized group or community. A community has purpose and plan, and there is in us an almost instinctive recognition of the connection between unity and strength.

Those who stand in disorganized masses against smaller groups of the organized are always aware of the tremendous odds against them. The sight of huge crowds of prisoners of war being herded toward collection centers by a few guards with rifles slung over their backs is one filled with pathos. It is not the absence of weapons that makes these prisoners helpless before their guards. It is the absence of a common will, the failing assurance that others will act in concert with you against the conquerors.

But organization is of many kinds, and the military kind is special in aiming at common and concrete goals. The organization of a civilian community, a city, for example, is not without goals, but they are rarely concrete, and many members are hardly aware of their existence. If a civilian community has goals with more reality and power to endure than military goals, as I believe it does, its goals are, nevertheless, unable to generate the degree of loyalty that a military organization can.

In war it is a commonplace of command that the goals of the fighting forces need to be clear and to be known. Naturally, the over-all goal is to win the war and then go home. But in any given action, the goal is to overcome the attacking enemy or, if you are the attacker, to win the stated objective. Any fighting unit must have a limited and specific objective, and the more defined and bounded it is, the greater the willingness, as a rule, on the part of soldiers to abandon their natural desire for self-preservation. Officers soon learn to dread hazy and ill-defined orders from above. If the goal is physical, a piece of earth to take or defend, a machine-gun nest to destroy, a strong point to annihilate, officers are much more likely to evoke the sense of comradeship. They realize that comradeship at first develops through the consciousness of an obstacle to be overcome through common effort. A fighting unit with morale is one in which many are of like mind and determination, unconsciously agreed on the suppression of individual desires in the interest of a shared purpose.

Organization for a common and concrete goal in peacetime organizations does not evoke anything like the degree of comradeship commonly known in war. Evidently, the presence of danger is distinctive and important. Men then are organized for a goal whose realization involves the real possibility of death or injury. How does danger break down the barriers of the self and give man an experience of community? The answer to this question is the key to one of the oldest and most enduring incitements to battle.

Danger provides a certain spice to experience; this is common knowledge. It quickens the pulse and makes us more aware of being alive by calling attention to our physical selves. The thrill of the chase in hunting, of riding a horse very fast, or of driving an automobile recklessly is of this sort. But the excitement created in us by such activities has little communal significance. Its origin appears to be sexual, if we understand sex in the wide sense given to it by Freud. The increased vitality we feel where danger is incidental is due to awareness of mastery over the environment. It is an individualist, not a communal, drive.

The excitement and thrill of battle, on the other hand, are of a different sort, for there danger is central and not incidental. There is little of the play element about combat, however much there may have been in training for it. Instead, for

43

most soldiers there is the hovering inescapable sense of ir-
reversibility. "This is for keeps," as soldier slang is likely to
put it. This profound earnestness is by no means devoid of
lightheartedness, as seen in teasing and horseplay, but men
are conscious that they are on a one-way street, so to speak,
and what they do or fail to do can be of great consequence.
Those who enter into battle, as distinguished from those who
only hover on its fringes, do not fight as duelists fight. Almost
automatically, they fight as a unit, a group. Training can help
a great deal in bringing this about more quickly and easily in
an early stage. But training can only help to make actual what
is inherent. As any commander knows, an hour or two of
combat can do more to weld a unit together than can months
of intensive training.

Many veterans who are honest with themselves will admit,
I believe, that the experience of communal effort in battle,
even under the altered conditions of modern war, has been a
high point in their lives. Despite the horror, the weariness, the
grime, and the hatred, participation with others in the chances
of battle had its unforgettable side, which they would not want
to have missed. For anyone who has not experienced it himself,
the feeling is hard to comprehend, and, for the participant,
hard to explain to anyone else. Probably the feeling of liberation is nearly basic. It is this feeling that explains the curious
combination of earnestness and lightheartedness so often noted
in men in battle.

Many of us can experience freedom as a thrilling reality,
something both serious and joyous, only when we are acting
in unison with others for a concrete goal that costs something
absolute for its attainment. Individual freedom to do what we
will with our lives and our talents, the freedom of self-de-
termination, appears to us most of the time as frivolous or

burdensome. Such freedom leaves us empty and alone, feeling undirected and insignificant. Only comparatively few of us know how to make this individual freedom productive and joyous. But communal freedom can pervade nearly everyone and carry everything before it. This elemental fact about freedom the opponents of democracy have learned well, and it constitutes for them a large initial advantage.

The lightheartedness that communal participation brings has little of the sensuous or merely pleasant about it, just as the earnestness has little of the calculating or rational. Both derive instead from a consciousness of power that is supra-individual. We feel earnest and gay at such moments because we are liberated from our individual impotence and are drunk with the power that union with our fellows brings. In moments like these many have a vague awareness of how isolated and separate their lives have hitherto been and how much they have missed by living in the narrow circle of family or a few friends. With the boundaries of the self expanded, they sense a kinship never known before. Their "I" passes insensibly into a "we," "my" becomes "our," and individual fate loses its central importance.

At its height, this sense of comradeship is an ecstasy not unlike the aesthetic ecstasy previously described, though occasioned by different forces. In most of us there is a genuine longing for community with our human species, and at the same time an awkwardness and helplessness about finding the way to achieve it. Some extreme experience—mortal danger or the threat of destruction—is necessary to bring us fully together with our comrades or with nature. This is a great pity, for there are surely alternative ways more creative and less dreadful, if men would only seek them out. Until now, war has appealed because we discover some of the mysteries of communal joy in its forbidden depths. Comradeship reaches its peak in battle.

The secret of comradeship has not been exhausted, however, in the feeling of freedom and power instilled in us by communal effort in combat. There is something more and equally important. The sense of power and liberation that comes over men at such moments stems from a source beyond the union of men. I believe it is nothing less than the assurance of immortality that makes self-sacrifice at these moments so relatively easy. Men are true comrades only when each is ready to give up his life for the other, without reflection and without thought of personal loss. Who can doubt that every war, the two world wars no less than former ones, has produced true comradeship like this?

Such sacrifice seems hard and heroic to those who have never felt communal ecstasy. In fact, it is not nearly so difficult as many less absolute acts in peacetime and in civilian life, for death becomes in a measure unreal and unbelievable to one who is sharing his life with his companions. Immortality is not something remote and otherworldly, possibly or probably true and real; on the contrary, it becomes a present and self-evident fact.

Nothing is further from the truth than the insistence of certain existentialist philosophers that each person must die his own death and experience it unsharably. If that were so, how many lives would have been spared on the battlefield! But in fact, death for men united with each other can be shared as few other of life's great moments can be. To be sure, it is not death as we know it usually in civilian life. In the German language men never die in battle. They *fall*. The term is exact for the expression of self-sacrifice when it is motivated by the feeling of comradeship. I may fall, but I do not die, for that which is real in me goes forward and lives on in the comrades for whom I gave up my physical life.

Let me not be misunderstood. It is unquestionably true that thousands of soldiers die in battle, miserable, alone, and embittered, without any conviction of self-sacrifice and without any other satisfactions. I suspect the percentage of such soldiers has increased markedly in recent wars. But for those who in every battle are seized by the passion for self-sacrifice, dying has lost its terrors because its reality has vanished.

There must be a similarity between this willingness of soldier-comrades for self-sacrifice and the willingness of saints and martyrs to die for their religious faith. It is probably no accident that the religions of the West have not cast away their military terminology or even their militant character— "Onward, Christian soldiers! Marching as to war . . ." nor that our wars are defended in terms of devotion and salvation. The true believer must be ready to give up his life for the faith. And if he is a genuine saint he will regard this sacrifice as no loss, for the self has become indestructible in being united with a supreme reality. There are, of course, important differences. The reality for which the martyr sacrifices himself is not visible and intimate like the soldier's. The martyr usually dies alone, scorned by the multitude. In this sense his lot is infinitely harder. It is hardly surprising that few men are capable of dying joyfully as martyrs whereas thousands are capable of self-sacrifice in wartime. Nevertheless, a basic point of resemblance remains, namely, that death has lost not only its sting but its reality, too, for the self that dies is little in comparison with that which survives and triumphs.

This is the mystical element of war that has been mentioned by nearly all serious writers on the subject. William James spoke of it as a sacrament, and once remarked that "society would rot without the mystical blood payment." And G. F. Nicolai, in his book *The Biology of War*, is persuaded that "the boundless capacity for self-sacrifice" is what is intoxicating and great about war. It is this that occasions frequent doubt in lovers of peace whether men will ever give up warfare, and, at times, the vagrant question whether it is desirable that they should. This capacity for self-sacrifice is what all defenders of war (in our day grown few) use as their final argument for the necessity and ultimate morality of war. Since men can only be brought by such extreme means to a recognition of their true nature and their essential relationships, these defenders tell us, it is folly to seek to abolish war, because it would be to abolish death itself.

Many humanists and humanitarians, on the other hand, attack the impulse to self-sacrifice as the very core of moral evil. It offends their whole rational image of the distinctively human. And the more forthright do not hesitate to express their abhorrence for the Christian faith insofar as it is founded on the theme of self-sacrifice. Readers of Rebecca West's *Black Lamb and Grey Falcon* will not easily forget the bitterness with which she deals with the notion of sacrifice and her rejection of Saint Paul, Saint Augustine, and Luther for burdening the Christian faith with "this ugly theme."

Her reflections, after witnessing a rather gruesome ceremony in the backwaters of Yugoslavia in which black lambs are sacrificed in the belief that they will heal the local peasants of sundry diseases, conclude as follows:

I knew this rock well. I had lived under the shadow of it all my life. All our Western thought is founded on this repulsive pretence that pain is the proper price of any good thing. Here it could be seen how the meaning of the Crucifixion had been hidden from us, though it was written clear. A supremely good man was born on earth, a man who was without cruelty, who could have taught mankind to live in perpetual happiness; and because we are infatuated with this idea of sacrifice, of shedding innocent blood to secure innocent advantages, we found nothing better to do with this passport to deliverance than to destroy him.

It is true that we in the West are frequently infatuated with the idea of sacrifice, particularly self-sacrifice. Why are some people so strongly repelled and others again and again attracted by the impulse to self-sacrifice? Or why do both attraction and repulsion have place in the same breast at different moments? As moralists, we are repelled, I suspect, because the impulse to sacrifice is not subject to rational judgment and control. It takes hold of us and forces us against our will, later claiming justification from some higher authority than the human. As often as not, it puts itself at the service of an evil cause, perhaps more frequently than in the service of the good. The mysterious power that such leaders as Napoleon, Hitler, and Stalin had in their being that enabled them to create a love for self-sacrifice perplexes us endlessly. We cannot condemn it with full conviction, since it seems likely that both leaders and led were in large degree powerless to prevent the impulses that dominated them.

Yet such power is appalling beyond measure and from a rational viewpoint deserving of the deepest condemnation. The limits of free will and morality are transgressed, and man is forced to seek religious and metaphysical justification for self-sacrifice, even when committed in an evil cause. As in the aesthetic appeal of war, when we reach the impulse of the sublime, so in the communal appeal of comradeship, when we reach the impulse to self-sacrifice, we are confronted with contradictions that are deeply embedded in our culture, if not in human nature itself. What our moral self tells us is abhorrent, our religious self and our aesthetic self yearn for as the ultimate good. This is part of the riddle of war.

If we are truly wise, perhaps we should not want to alter these capacities of our human nature, even though we suffer from them immeasurably and may yet succumb to their threat. For the willingness to sacrifice self, like the attraction of the sublime, is what makes possible the higher reaches of the spirit into the realms of poetry, philosophy, and genuine religion. They prevent our best men from losing interest in and hope for our species. They stand in the way of discouragement and cynicism. As moralists, we can condemn Saint Paul and Saint Augustine for their mystical conviction that without sacrifice no purgation from sin is possible. But we should be cautious in so doing, for they were convinced that without the supra-moral act, we human beings are not able to lead even a normally moral existence. Though they were not disposed to believe that God was without moral qualities, they were quite certain that there was more in His universe than the determinations of good and evil. For them the "I am" preceded logically and in time the "I ought." And vast numbers of people have agreed with them that the religious order is superior to the moral, though they continue to be confused about how the two are related.

Are we not right in honoring the fighter's impulse to sacrifice himself for a comrade, even though it be done, as it so frequently is, in an evil cause? I think so. It is some kind of world historical pathos that the striving for union and for immortality must again and again be consummated while men are in the service of destruction. I do not doubt for a moment that wars are made many times more deadly because of this striving and this impulse. Yet I would not want to be without the assurance their existence gives me that our species has a different destiny than is granted to other animals. Though we often sink below them, we can at moments rise above them, too.

If the lust of the eye and the yearning for communion with our fellows were the only appeals of combat, we might be confident that they would be ultimately capable of satisfaction in other ways. But my own observation and the history of warfare both convince me that there is a third impulse to battle much more sinister than these. Anyone who has watched men on the battlefield at work with artillery, or looked into the eyes of veteran killers fresh from slaughter, or studied the descriptions of bombardiers' feelings while smashing their targets, finds hard to escape the conclusion that there is a delight in destruction. A walk across any battlefield shortly after the guns have fallen silent is convincing enough. A sensitive person is sure to be oppressed by a spirit of evil there, a radical evil which suddenly makes the medieval images of hell and the thousand devils of that imagination believable. This evil appears to surpass mere human malice and to demand explanation in cosmological and religious terms.

Men who have lived in the zone of combat long enough to be veterans are sometimes possessed by a fury that makes them capable of anything. Blinded by the rage to destroy and supremely careless of consequences, they storm against the enemy until they are either victorious, dead, or utterly exhausted. It is as if they are seized by a demon and are no longer in control of themselves. From the Homeric account of the sacking of Troy to the conquest of Dienbienphu, Western literature is filled with descriptions of soldiers as berserkers and mad destroyers.

Perhaps the following account from the diary of Ernst

51

Juenger in World War I may stand for many because it is so concise and exactly drawn. It describes the beginning of the last German offensive in the West.

The great moment had come. The curtain of fire lifted from the front trenches. We stood up.

With a mixture of feelings, evoked by bloodthirstiness, rage, and intoxication, we moved in step, ponderously but irresistibly toward the enemy lines. I was well ahead of the company, followed by Vinke and a one-year veteran named Haake. My right hand embraced the shaft of my pistol, my left a riding stick of bamboo cane. I was boiling with a mad rage, which had taken hold of me and all the others in an incomprehensible fashion. The overwhelming wish to kill gave wings to my feet. Rage pressed bitter tears from my eyes.

The monstrous desire for annihilation, which hovered over the battlefield, thickened the brains of the men and submerged them in a red fog. We called to each other in sobs and stammered disconnected sentences. A neutral observer might have perhaps believed that we were seized by an excess of happiness.

Happiness is doubtless the wrong word for the satisfaction that men experience when they are possessed by the lust to destroy and to kill their kind. Most men would never admit that they enjoy killing, and there are a great many who do not. On the other hand, thousands of youths who never suspected the presence of such an impulse in themselves have learned in military life the mad excitement of destroying. The appetite is one that requires cultivation in the environment of disorder and deprivation common to life at the front. It usually marks the great difference between green troops and veterans. Generals often name it "the will to close with the enemy." This innocent-sounding phrase conceals the very substance of the delight in destruction slumbering in most of us. When soldiers step over the line that separates self-defense from fighting for its own sake, as it is so easy for them to do, they experience something that stirs deep chords in their being. The soldier-killer is learning to serve a different deity, and his concern is with death and not life, destruction and not construction.

Of the many writers who are preoccupied today with man's urge toward destruction, Ernest Hemingway stands out as one who has succeeded in incorporating the spirit of violence in his men and women. In his *For Whom the Bell Tolls,* he has his hero say at one point: "Stop making dubious literature about the Berbers and the old Iberians and admit that you have liked to kill as all who are soldiers by choice have enjoyed it at some time whether they lie about it or not." And his old colonel in the more recent book *Across the River and into the Trees* is as profound a portrait of the soldier-killer as we have seen in recent literature. The colonel is so far aware of this impulse to destruction in himself that he tries to counterbalance it by the contrary appeal, namely, Eros, in the form of the young and beautiful countess. This latter book has been harshly criticized from an artistic point of view, and not many have seen, I believe, how well Hemingway grasps the two primordial forces that are in conflict within the colonel, as within many a professional warrior, conflicts that can be resolved in a fashion only by death.

Sigmund Freud has labeled these forces in human nature the Eros drive or instinct, the impulse within us that strives for closer union with others and seeks to preserve and conserve, and the Thanatos (death) drive or instinct, the impulse that works for the dissolution of everything living or united. Freud felt that these two are in eternal conflict within man, and he became, consequently, pessimistic about ever eradicating war as an institution. Men are in one part of their being in love with death, and periods of war in human society represent the dominance of this impulsion.

Of course, this idea of an independent destructive force in life is age-old. The early Greek philosopher Empedocles gave imaginative form to a cosmology in which two universal principles explain the universe. Empedocles taught that the universe is in ceaseless change, in generation and decay, because Love and Strife are ever at work in the animate and the inanimate. Love unites all forms of life, for a period holding the upper hand, and Strife tears them apart and breaks down what previously belonged together. The original components are not annihilated, but simply dispersed in various forms by Strife. They are able to form new unions once more, and the endless process of composition and decomposition continues. Empedocles conceived both forces as of equal strength, both eternal, and both mixed equally in all things. In this imaginative vision of the world process, he sees, also, a necessary relationship between these cosmological powers, an insight that is sounder and more fruitful than most modern conceptions.

We are tempted under the influence of Darwinian thought to explain away man's delight in destruction as a regressive impulse, a return to primitivism and to animal nature. We picture, sometimes with the help of Freudians, all our cultural institutions as a kind of mask covering up the animalistic instincts that lie beneath the surface of all behavior. Such a view tends to explain all phenomena of human destructiveness, from the boyish pleasure in the tinkle of broken glass to the sadistic orgies of concentration camps, as a reassertion of man's animal nature under the veneer of culture. Man when he destroys is an animal; when he conserves he is distinctively human.

I cannot escape the conviction that this is an illusion, and a dangerous one. When man is at his destructive work, he is on a different plane from the animal altogether. And destructive urges are as capable of being found in highly cultivated natures as in the simpler ones, if not more so. The satisfaction in destroying seems to me peculiarly human, or, more exactly put, devilish in a way animals can never be. We sense in it always the Mephistophelean cry that all created things deserve to be destroyed. Sometimes there is no more concrete motive for destroying than this one, just as there is no expressible motive for creating. I described this kind of wanton behavior in my journal one night.

It was an unforgivable spectacle. They shamed us as Americans, as colleagues and junior officers, they shamed us before our hired people. Our President lay on his bier in Washington, boys from our Division lay wounded and dying on the battlefields round about, and these lordly colonels drank themselves senseless and wantonly destroyed property with their pistols. It was a commentary on the war, on the uselessness of fighting for ideals, on the depravity of the military life.

Indeed, there are many important similarities, I feel, between the creative and destructive urges in most of us. Surely the immediate sense of release that is the satisfaction in accomplishment and mastery is not very different in the two impulses. One may become a master in one field as in the other, and there are perhaps as many levels of accomplishment. Few men ever reach superlatives in the realm of destruction; most of us remain, as in the domain of creation, moderately capable.

But artistry in destruction is qualitatively different in its effects upon the individual, in a way that minimizes similarities. It loosens one by one our ties with others and leaves us in the end isolated and alone. Destruction is an artistry directed not toward perfection and fulfillment, but toward chaos and moral anarchy. Its delights may be deep and within the reach of more men than are the joys of creation, but their capacity to reproduce and to endure is very limited. Just as creation raises us above the level of the animal, destruction forces us below it by eliminating communication. As creativity can unite us with our natural and human environment, destruction isolates us from both. That is why destruction in retrospect usually appears so repellent in its inmost nature.

If we ask what the points of similarity are between the appeal of destruction and the two appeals of war I have already examined, I think it is not difficult to recognize that the delight in destroying has, like the others, an ecstatic character. But in one sense only. Men feel overpowered by it, seized from without, and relatively helpless to change or control it. Nevertheless, it is an ecstasy without a union, for comradeship among killers is terribly difficult, and the kinship with nature that aesthetic vision often affords is closed to them. Nor is the breaking down of the barriers of self a quality of the appeal of destroying. On the contrary, I think that destruction is ultimately an individual matter, a function of the person and not the group. This is not to deny, of course, that men go berserk in groups and kill more easily together than when alone. Yet the satisfaction it brings appears to lie, not in losing themselves and their egos, but precisely in greater consciousness of themselves. If they hold together as partners in destruction, it is not so much from a feeling of belonging as from fear of retaliation when alone.

The willingness to sacrifice self for comrades is no longer characteristic of soldiers who have become killers for pleasure. War henceforth becomes for them increasingly what the philosopher Hobbes thought to be the primal condition of all human life, a war of every man against every man. That soldier-killers seldom reach this stage must be attributed to the presence of other impulses in their nature and to the episodical character of battle and combat. I can hardly doubt that the delight in destruction leads in this direction.

This is not the only melancholy consequence of this impulse, for its very nature is to be totalitarian and exclusive. Unlike other delights, it becomes, relatively soon in most men, a consuming lust which swallows up other pleasures. It tends to turn men inward upon themselves and make them inaccessible to more normal satisfactions. Because they rarely can feel remorse, they experience no purgation and cannot grow. The utter absence of love in this inverted kind of creation makes the delight essentially sterile. Though there may be a fierce pride in the numbers destroyed and in their reputation for proficiency, soldier-killers usually experience an ineffable sameness and boredom in their lives. The restlessness of such men in rest areas behind the front is notorious.

How deeply is this impulse to destroy rooted and persistent in human nature? Are the imaginative visions of Empedocles and Freud true in conceiving that the destructive element in man and nature is as strong and recurrent as the conserving, erotic element? Or can our delight in destruction be channeled into other activities than the traditional one of warfare? We are not far advanced on the way to these answers. We do not know whether a peaceful society can be made attractive enough to wean men away from the appeals of battle. Today we are seeking to make war so horrible that men will be frightened away from it. But this is hardly likely to be more fruitful in the future than it has been in the past. More productive will certainly be our efforts to eliminate the social, economic, and political injustices that are always the immediate occasion of hostilities. Even then, we shall be confronted with the spiritual emptiness and inner hunger that impel many men toward combat. Our society has not begun to wrestle with this problem of how to provide fulfillment to human life, to which war is so often an illusory path.

The weather has been unspeakably bad also, and what with the dawning realization that the war may continue through the winter, it has been sufficient to lower my previous high spirits. Perhaps "high spirits" is not the proper term for the nervous excitement and tension of this war front. I experience so much as in a dream or as on a stage, and at times I can step aside, as one does in a dream, and say: Is this really I? "Sad and laughable and strange" is the best combination of adjectives to describe these twilight days of our old world—the words that Plato used to describe his great myth at the end of The Republic. *I would say, first strange, then sad, then laughable—but the laugh is not the same as the laugh of one in love when his beloved has delighted him with some idiosyncrasy of love. It is the laugh of the fallen angels who have renounced heaven but find hell hard to endure. (War journal, October 2, 1944)*

LOVE:

WAR'S

ALLY

AND FOE

. . . the Greeks were wise men when they mated the god of war with the goddess Aphrodite. The soldier must not only kill, he must give birth to new warriors. (A letter to a friend, August 28, 1944, from southern France)

In my journal I find no description of a cave in one of Italy's most despoiled towns where the whole population was forced to spend several days while the front passed. Why I did not record an incident that happened to me there, I do not know, possibly because I thought it incomprehensible. On the chance that German deserters or Fascist partisans might be concealed among the civilian populace, I decided to inspect this cave. The exploration was the nearest thing to a journey in Dante's *Inferno* that I was to know in the war. Each family group had tried to establish a tiny living space in the dank, unlighted dungeon where one had constantly to stoop to avoid the dirt roof. The only light came from various small fires and the occasional candles of those families who had had the foresight to bring a few provisions with them. Because there was no ventilation, no water, no toilet facilities, the stench was nearly unendurable.

I stumbled and groped my way forward, trying to avoid stepping on bodies, afraid I would faint from lack of oxygen. Acrid smoke burned my eyes and made it difficult to avoid collision with hundreds lying, sitting, or crouching about on all sides. Children were screaming, old men and women coughing or moaning, while others tried to prepare some gruel over smoking coals. Far back in the cave, which seemed never-ending, I struck my head against the roof and slipped to my knees. My hand, thrown out to steady me, touched not the filthy floor but the fingers and palm of a woman's hand, quickly raised to prevent my falling on her. In the darkness I could discern only a half-recumbent form directly beneath me. Mumbling an apology I hastily withdrew my hand, but not before I felt a responsive clasp from hers, unmistakably amorous.

At the entrance and in the fresh air at last, I held my splitting head in my hands and slowly recovered from the foulness. But to understand how anyone in this situation could possibly feel desire was completely beyond me. In the perspective of memory, however, this incident may well be taken as symbolical of the curious affinities between love and war.

There is a familiar Greek myth about the goddess of love, Aphrodite, becoming the mistress of Ares, god of war, whose youth and passion captured her heart, though she was the bride of Hephaestos, who forged the weapons and armor of the gods. The two of them spent many sweet, illicit hours together, and one of their children was the beautiful Harmonia, another the ever-youthful Eros. This liaison between love and war, familiar early in Western history, might occasion more wonder and reflection than it usually does. How can it be that these two, outwardly so unlike, have any attraction for each other at all? What is the source of this affinity? Is the attraction really an adulterous one, as in the myth, or is it more legitimate than the early Greeks wanted to believe? How durable can we expect this liaison to be between love and war? Questions like these arise almost spontaneously when I begin to reflect on modern enactments of the Aphrodite-Ares story in World War II.

Anyone entering military service for the first time can only be astonished by soldiers' concentration upon the subject of women and, more especially, upon the sexual act. The most common word in the mouths of American soldiers has been the vulgar expression for sexual intercourse. This word does duty as adjective, adverb, verb, noun, and in any other form it can possibly be used, however inappropriate or ridiculous in application. Many soldiers seem hardly able to utter a sentence without using it at least once. Apparently they derive a vague satisfaction by invoking the word itself, habitual and thoughtless as its employment becomes. It must serve to recall fleeting memories or fond desires. At all events, its overuse indicates clearly a predominant interest for nearly all military men in wartime.

If we are honest, most of us who were civilian soldiers in recent wars will confess that we spent incomparably more time in the service of Eros during our military careers than ever before or again in our lives. When we were in uniform almost any girl who was faintly attractive had an erotic appeal for us. For their part, millions of women find a strong sexual attraction in the military uniform, particularly in time of war. This fact is as inexplicable as it is notorious. Many a girl who had hitherto led a casual and superficial existence within a protective family circle has been suddenly overwhelmed by intense passion for a soldier met by chance on the street or at a dance for servicemen. It seems that the very atmosphere of large cities in wartime breathes the enticements of physical love. Not only are inhibitions on sexual expression lowered, but there exists a much more passionate interest of the sexes in each other than is the case in peacetime. Men and women normally absorbed by other concerns find themselves caught up in the whirlpool of erotic love, which is the preoccupation of the day. In wartime marriages multiply and the birth rate increases. We can safely assume that the number of love affairs, if they could be reduced to statistics, would show an even greater rate of expansion.

I find it hard to accept the usual sociological and psychological explanations of this phenomenon, though they must be true in part. Sociologists fasten upon the uprooting character of war experience. War always signifies an artificial separation of the sexes or, at best, a maldistribution. The soldier is torn loose from his home moorings and community context, and exposed to worry, threats, isolation, and loneliness. In an unfriendly male environment he yearns for the protective, orderly existence that is symbolized by women and home. Preoccupation with sex becomes a form of compensation for what he has lost; it is an expression of his maladjustment. A healthy interest in sex is likely only when the individual moves in his own social sphere. Undoubtedly, a great deal of wartime love can be ascribed in part to the loss of our proper environment. What is not explained, however, is why women whose external lives have not been greatly deranged by war are equally subject to love's fever. Evidently other and deeper forces are involved as well.

Biological psychologists are fond of reminding us that civilized controls over sex impulses impose a severe strain on the psyche. War offers us an opportunity to return to nature and to look upon every member of the opposite sex as a possible conquest, to be wooed or forced. For such a view, Ares and Aphrodite are kindred gods who need and understand each other. Both are under the control, however, of some larger evolutionary principle, usually called the struggle for existence or the will to live. Because war poses a special threat to the survival of the species, this principle calls up in the individual members unconscious but powerful counterforces. We reproduce our kind more rapidly because we are also engaged in destroying other members of the species. As individuals we have no freedom to do otherwise, since the needs of the species are imperious. As one of nature's numerous progeny, we are subject to the same laws as the rest.

Love in wartime does have a compulsiveness about it that peacetime seldom knows. It falls upon us "like a mountain wind upon an oak, shaking us leaf and bough," in the striking simile of the poet Sappho. It overleaps national boundaries and overcomes obstacles that at other times might appear insuperable. Nevertheless, the biological basis of this love is transformed by its human qualities and becomes something other than the urge to reproduce. The determinism we experience in love stems not alone from nature, but is an intimate determinism arising out of our gift of freedom. There is doubtless truth in the naturalistic claim that forces are at work in war and love that we rarely make conscious and never completely understand. But these forces are not merely biological; on the contrary, they are distinctively human as well.

63

Love has many levels, and we use the same word to cover a multitude of relationships between two human beings, relationships that are different but not separable from each other. Even erotic love between men and women where sexual need appears to be the foundation of the relationship has, as everyone knows, a thousand nuances. Reflection upon war experience in relation to love has convinced me of this, at least, that the liaison between the gods of love and of war rests at some levels upon the attraction of opposites, at others upon their essential kinship. Neither Ares nor Aphrodite is a simple or a simple-minded god, and their union is no easy thing to comprehend. Of the various kinds of love that determine men at war, which are called forth by and are kin to war and which, opposed to destruction and death, may become the instruments of peace?

I have observed three distinct kinds of love operating during war. They are erotic love between the sexes, preservative love, which is independent of sex distinctions, and the love called friendship. These loves are, of course, not unknown to peace. But in times of strife they are sometimes more clearly defined, and the ornamentations in which love abounds are more likely to be stripped away. War has its own conventions, to be sure, and it quickly camouflages true relations and original impulses among human creatures. Yet there are moments of lucidity, even terrible clarity, which can be enlightening when we succeed in re-creating them in memory without distortion.

For many soldiers of World War II, love between the sexes appeared to be nothing else than an outlet in the purely physical sense, which physiologists of love are fond of describing. There was an unmistakable similarity in it to eating and drinking, a devouring of the woman as object. Even the appetite seemed to recur with the same regularity as do hunger and thirst. To these soldiers it did not much matter who the woman was they used to satisfy themselves. Their claims on her were only on her external features, so that prostitutes gave such soldiers as much as any other girl could, and were usually much more in accord with military needs. It is not at all surprising that many army commanders have over the centuries sought to organize love by providing legal brothels for soldiers. From a narrow military standpoint, these establishments have always appeared to limit the dangers of physical love and insure efficiency of soldiering.

It is not easy to grasp the full coarseness of this gross physical love. Those who are repelled by the descriptions of it some soldiers like to give are accustomed to class it as bestial and animalistic without reflecting upon it further. In the memories and imaginations of these soldiers, women were reduced not only to objects, but to sexual organs which they could manipulate to their complete satisfaction. There was little or no tenderness in their passion, and gentleness in its expression was a thing unknown. The sexual need of these soldiers appeared to lie so near the surface as to be associated with only one part of their being. To put it more exactly, the need appeared to be separable as a passion that shook them from without and at intervals only. Such soldiers could not be called sensualists, for they knew little about the real pleasures of physical love. Their passion was too external and superficial for that.

For a time during the war in France, I was closely associated with an officer to whom love was purely an external appetite. His favorite expression was that he was a man who could not sleep alone. In fact, he usually found a girl to share his bed, and frequently several different girls in the course of a week. Yet it was apparent to those of us who knew him well that these relationships gave momentary satisfaction only. Despite his highly developed capacity for physical love, he knew extremely little about making the act more pleasurable for himself. It would never have occurred to him to cultivate affection for some of his many girls as a way of increasing his pleasure. So far as I could tell, he derived his greatest satisfaction from recounting his conquests to any of us who would listen. The girls he conquered sustained his ego and persuaded him that he was more than adequate as a lover.

I do not need to furnish any further description of this level of erotic love. Any veteran who reads these lines will have a thousand memories of it, personal or vicarious. Even those who escaped much contact with such love know well enough its appeal and realize that we are not separated from it by any absolute barrier. Fastidiousness, moral restraint, or the habit of treating the opposite sex as human beings may prohibit sympathy for soldiers such as these. But there is enough of the rapist in every man to give him insight into the grossest manifestations of sexual passion. Hence it is presumptuous for any of us to scorn the practitioners of this lowest kind of passion as beings with whom we have no kinship.

Surely this kind of love is intimately associated with the impersonal violence of war. Ares and Aphrodite here attract one another as true mates. Copulation under such circumstances is an act of aggression; the girl is the victim and her conquest the victor's triumph. Preliminary resistance on her part always increases his satisfaction, since victory is more intoxicating the harder the winning may be. It is not without significance that the language of physical love and the language of battle have a large correspondence, and the phrase "the war of the sexes" can be rich in connotation. Love like this can be as cruel as battle, because it arises from one part of the human being only, a part that is sundered from the whole.

That we can respond with only one aspect of our total selves is the frightening quality of our human life. Far from being weaker, this abstract response is usually more virulent and violent than response by the whole person. It seems hardly necessary to remark that such degradation is not possible for other than the human species. The animal cannot transform his mate into an object because it does not regard itself as a subject. A human being who thus deserts his humanity does not become like an animal, but, in the expressive German term, an *Untier* (an "unanimal"), in an exact sense, a creature without parallel in nature. The conquest of the sexual partner thus becomes very like the conquest of the enemy, who has forfeited any right to human status or equality. I described this experience in my journal one day:

Stories are constantly brought to us of the Moroccan soldiers raping women and children, robbing and pillaging, and generally terrorizing the Italians. Just an hour ago, a group of Italians came to the PW cage, where I am working, with fearful stories of how their small daughters are taken to the woods and violated by these French Moroccan soldiers. I spoke to the MP officer in charge about it. He said, "There is nothing we can do. The complaints have been taken to the French General in charge, who merely laughed and said, 'This is war.' We cannot control these soldiers or convince them that the Italians are not their enemies when a year or two ago the Italians were doing the same thing in Africa." . . . The incident made me wonder about the idea of kindness in culture, made me remember how the Greeks, highly cultured Athenians, were heartlessly cruel to their enemies, yet preserved their own humanity. . . . Perhaps humanitarianism needs to be reconsidered and re-evaluated. An interesting study

67

would be the growth of the idea of humanitarianism and, related to it, the idea of sadism. Because sadism is an antithesis of everything humanitarianism signifies, it should be correlated with it.

It would be folly, I believe, to minimize the similarity between war and this gross form of love. Observation of others and being honest about our own sensations must convince us that sexual passion in isolation and the lust for battle are closely akin. Such sexual passion and war have been married from the beginning, and there is no cause to speak of an illicit relationship. To be sure, the sexual partner is not actually destroyed in the encounter, merely overthrown. And the psychological aftereffects of sexual lust are different from those of battle lusts. These differences, however, do not alter the fact that the passions have a common source and affect their victims in the same way while they are in their grip. We should not forget, either, that sometimes the consequences are not so different, after all. Sexual lust often leads to murder, and in wartime, particularly, the same person often suffers rape and murder. Both reveal man as a berserker, outside of his humanity, a dangerous beast of prey.

There is another level of love in which Ares and Aphrodite are at one in sympathy, but here the specifically human element is present. I refer to the thoroughgoing sensualist. Many a soldier has learned all the physiological and psychological delights of erotic love while remaining blind to its higher satisfactions. For such a soldier, love is an appetite, closely associated in fact with eating and drinking, but far superior to them, since it yields both a more pervasive and intense kind of pleasure. Eating and drinking become for him preliminary stages; they are put in the service of his supreme earthly bliss. His dreams are of romantic conquests in which the final act of physical release is preceded by lengthy seduction byplay.

Though selfish to the core, the sensualist possesses real tenderness in his love-making, and he strives for his girl's satisfaction as the most delightful part of his own. Unlike the coarser soldier, whom he scorns, he is selective. His girls must be refined enough to conceal and help him cover up the less attractive aspects of physical passion. His promiscuity is tempered by the recognition that a love partner can only be properly enjoyed when time is given to develop tenderness and affection on both sides. He is not inclined to overlook her humanity, though that is not an end for him but a means. A sensualist looks at every attractive woman as a possible conquest. She is for him of interest solely because of her sex. And he regards himself as a male before he thinks of himself as a human being. In memory he luxuriates in comparisons of this or that ladylove with others, recalling the distinctive refinements of his various loves. Girls are for him gorgeous creatures, instruments on which he strives to play with infinite skill and patience.

For the sensualist as soldier, war is not only a convenient opportunity for new and wider fields of erotic conquest; the violence associated with it corresponds to something deeply implanted in his nature. He can be, and often is, the most refined sadist in dealing with helpless enemy soldiers. He is capable of fierce anger and is likely to be the most unrelenting exponent of brute force in solving all problems of war. The surprising thing about the sensualistic soldier is that his erotic experiences have no softening effect on his personality. If anything, they appear to harden him. The tenderness he displays toward his girl of the moment turns to harshness and cruelty toward men under his control or toward the captured enemy. I can only conclude that for the sensualist, as for his coarser brother, love signifies a devouring of the object and not a union with the subject. The beauty of loving is for him an outer cloak only; inwardly he is either empty or rapacious. Moreover, he is essentially uncontrollable by reason; his nature is in the service of passion exclusively.

The deities of love and war have never given birth to more dangerous offspring than these complete sensualists. Mythologically, they are the children of Anteros (Passion), who was also a son of the union of Ares and Aphrodite. These soldiers make war with the same participation of their whole being as they make love. The absence of external coarseness and obscenity in them is a poor compensation for the increased possibilities of degradation and genuine wickedness they display. Sensualists usually have complex natures, and frequently intelligent ones as well. Since they are given over to passions of love and violence, they live in war's element more internally secure than anyone else. It is as though they find in the union of love and war the only fulfillment of which they are capable. Unlike the simpler soldier already described, whose sexual needs appear relatively external and separable from the rest of him, the sensualists are integral; they are whole men in the expression of their passions. Hence they can more easily step over the line to become killers and to delight in destruction for its own sake than any other kind of soldier. Fewer inhibitions restrain them and their interests are usually narrow, being concentrated on conquest, erotic or martial.

But, a skeptical reader may ask, are there such soldiers in reality or is this not an abstraction you are depicting? I confess that I have never known a complete sensualist before or since my army days and so can understand a reader's doubts. Perhaps it is because I have moved in more restricted circles, as most of us do in civilian life. Sensualists thrive in peace-time, no doubt, but their nature of necessity is more concealed and their desires disguised by interests of business and commerce. But that undisguised sensualists exist in every combat unit, nearly every former soldier with any perception can testify.

For other soldiers at war, the erotic appeal is evidently in contrast with the ugly realities of combat. Ares and Aphrodite attract as opposites and not as soul mates. Such soldiers long for the gentleness and affection that only women can bring into the very male character of martial existence. Physical need might well be a basis of this love, and sensuous excitement its very breath, but its sweetness and beauty make it memorable and worthy. A soldier who feels this may not know what it is that stirs him so profoundly about a girl's presence, but he surmises dimly that it is her presence itself and not merely her body that moves him. It is the feminine quality of being that he unconsciously wants to fulfill him. Physical and spiritual elements are so fused in his desire that they are indistinguishable.

In the battle areas of World War II, there was something indescribably poignant about many such love liaisons. Plain and commonplace as the women might be under normal circumstances, they appeared as angels of beauty and tenderness to combat soldiers starved for these qualities. More often than not, the soldier and his newly found sweetheart understood little or nothing of each other's language. But the inability to communicate and the strangeness of different customs appeared to heighten the joy of discovery for them. The brevity and often stolen character of their love gave every incident a special imprint on the memory. Those tingling guarded memories of tenderness and beauty were frequently sufficient to preserve the courage of the soldier and strengthen him for the return to battle. To have a yielding, caressing girl in his arms after hideous or nondescript days and nights in battle was to have impossibly much when he had got used to so little.

Here the physical relationship was frequently veiled by an all-encompassing tenderness, and came to seem, in their need of each other, an incident only. Almost of necessity there was much illusion in this love. The soldier who returned after the war to marry his sweetheart of a night or two often found heartache and disillusion, as the statistics of such marriages reveal, for the attraction on both sides was too obviously a product of the immediate situation and the war. Another soldier or another girl under similar conditions might have satisfied as well the need for affection and physical love. For the soldier who did not return, his memories remain unsullied and inextinguishable.

A love like this has for relatively uncorrupted natures a wonderfully beneficent effect as a counterpoise to the impersonal slaughter around them. Transient though it may be, and much less individual than either the soldier or his girl will admit, their love has the power to conserve the precious qualities of their being. These qualities are the most widely shared and most generally human that our species knows. For men and women who are cast about in time and space by the fortunes of war, no other response is left than to find occasional loves and to pour into them all their longing for beauty and gentleness and charm. Moralists should not quarrel about the nonspecific character of this love; hence its transience and the illusions it cherishes. Of all wartime loves, it is likely, possibly, to be most moral in its effects. Without loves like these, the human spirit would be much slower in recuperating from the psychical wounds of conflict. Indeed, many would never recover at all.

. . . and because you are a good friend I can risk telling you of a wonderful "femme fatale" in my recent experience. By a series of chance circumstances we were thrown together, why and how and wherefore I hardly know. The girl comes from a good family, has everything in the world, and is, quite objectively speaking, enchantingly beautiful.

A hundred times she said to me in her quaint and hesitant English: "I am happy," or in her liquid French: "Je suis content," and I laughed each time like a man whose eyes have been opened after years of darkness. After a thousand forced, sardonic, or self-conscious laughs, there is the laugh of pure joy, of unconscious, uninhibited delight in beauty and freedom. "Where hushed awakenings are dear . . ." In the night a German plane came over, there was flak, she stirred in my arms, awoke, and was a little frightened, crept closer in my arms, whispered dear words. I blessed the plane and could not have been frightened had the hotel shaken under bombs.

And because you must laugh at me and at this experience a little, I shall tell you that since knowing her my lips and ears have been opened in French and I can now understand the language and make myself understood in it! It is amazing what two nights can do when one has to make oneself understood. She would say the same about English.

Shall I tell you why I believe such an experience is given to me at such a time as this? At this you must not laugh. To give me strength and courage to bear the present and the near future, when we enter Germany and must endure horrible things. I think these events are heaven-directed and instilled with purpose and meaning. I shall henceforth be less willing in difficult times "to curse God and die," a little more certain that I have something to perform in the world. As life becomes more disordered and a waste over here, and there are only memories to sustain us, how important it is to have pure memories, strong, sweet, eternal memories.

Still other soldiers find in war erotic love that goes deeper than the appeals of tenderness and beauty, love that fills them completely and is painfully specific and individual, painfully, because such love is exposed to the arbitrariness of bullets and bombs in a cruel way and painfully, too, because this love is no respecter of persons and frequently chooses archenemies as its unhappy principals. How often in recent wars has the tragedy of Romeo and Juliet been re-enacted, without benefit of Shakespeare's lyric music to moderate the agony! To the lovers, their love appears to be independent of and unrelated to the war and all its madness. Their love is written in the stars and not in the march orders and manipulations of a military headquarters. They would have met and found each other had the war never been. If in fact their attachment is not so dissevered from the abysses of war as they think, the principals are quite certain that its issue is all that really matters. Their passionate recognition that they belong together causes them to disregard every claim to their allegiance that conflicts with their love. Loyalty to country and comrades, to family and to established habits of life, cannot withstand the demands and claims of such a relationship.

In France in 1944, as our forces liberated town after town from the Germans, many of us were unwilling spectators of unforgettable scenes. The French Resistance forces insisted on a public shaving of the heads of those girls who had had German lovers during the Occupation. This gruesome ceremony was commonly performed on a platform in the public square, and was attended by a numerous, sometimes mocking, crowd. A good number of the girls were evidently prostitutes, and their shearing was a spectacle only, unpleasant for an outsider to behold, satisfying for the French who had lived and suffered under the threat of being informed upon as underground workers by girls like these. But where the girl had been genuinely in love with her foreign soldier, the scene took on an uncanny character, producing in many of us a deep unease. I thought that French faces in the crowd of onlookers betrayed all the contradictions implicit in the drama. Presumably, the French, better than other nations, understood the nature of love and realized that national boundaries cannot contain or restrain it. They recognized that their young men of the Resistance were punishing, by attempting to shame publicly, girls who could not have done other than what they did. As such, this was an act of injustice, and not to be taken lightly by Frenchmen, even though commonplace enough in war. But as passionate political partisans they found it incredible that a truly French girl could have traffic with one of the hated enemy. A love that set all national and familial virtues at naught, a love that defied the claims of fatherland and natural loyalties must be monstrous and deserving of the punishment being meted out. No matter how erect and proud a girl might stand on the platform before her tormentors, and regardless of her reputed good character in other ways, she must conceal within her being some evil stain. Thus I chose to interpret the strange and baffled expressions on the faces of some of the quieter and more sensitive bystanders.

It is hard for anyone reading about these events, in a comfortable armchair far removed in time and space from their reality, to experience any of the desolation of spirit they inspired in some of us. Evil was not triumphing over good in the usual sense, for the FFI youths and their families had suffered cruelly from this enemy whom they felt to be at war with all mankind. In most cases, the girl herself did not approve of either the German nation or its policies in France. She felt herself to be a passionate defender of French ideals and French democracy. But . . . her lover was different. He was not one of the hated enemy, though he wore their uniform, spoke their language, and was forced to obey their commands. His soul was not foreign; it was free of all contagion by the alien and hostile, for it belonged to her completely. She could look out upon her townspeople and persecutors with a certain pity, not unmixed with scorn, because only she knew what a gulf separated her from them. The shudder that went through me at such sights was called forth by a premonition that the punishment was not only unjust, but also unholy. This love of hers was not only uncontrollable, it was a blessing, and to punish one of the principals was to play, unwittingly or not, a satanic role.

There was, of course, nothing specifically French about manifestations like this. Later, many of us were to see in Germany that a girl could love an Allied soldier who was fighting and killing her brothers or father. And the soldier could love her in return and genuinely hate her people. Separated and estranged from everyone but each other, these lovers felt secure and morally impregnable, though their fates might tomorrow become unbearably hard. Other lands must also have witnessed similar scenes in recent wars. In fact, they must have happened in most wars in Western history, if war literature can be trusted. Many happy marriages have been consummated between former enemies where the husband has been the slayer of his wife's closest relatives. The theme sounds primitive and archaic enough, something from the early sagas, but it is no doubt as contemporary as the war raging somewhere today.

Few of us can comprehend the mystery of this love. We

see Ares and Aphrodite mated and so well mated that their child might well be named Harmonia. At the same time the world lies in ruins around them, not only physically but morally, too, for their union tears apart the firmest beliefs in the worth of family, nation, and the whole complex of inherited tradition.

Yet we may well ask whether this love of a man and a woman for each other in which both have their whole being is really a mating of love and war. Is not war in this case an absurd accompaniment only? What can war and tragedy give this love that it would not have in time of peace? Certainly such love takes place in peace and among fellow countrymen more commonly than among members of opposed nations. Hence it does not require perverse outer circumstances for its fulfillment. Nevertheless, the presence of danger and the threat of separation do add something in the way of perfection or completeness, perhaps the realization of good fortune in having found the true love.

Too many of us as yet are so constituted that we cannot gain under peaceful skies an awareness of our own nature and the possibility of its union with another. When death and deprivation lurk near at hand, and only then, can many of us summon the necessary seriousness and wisdom, the necessary joy, to recognize love's true form. Genuine love can hardly actualize itself in Utopia, and certainly cannot there produce an awareness of its nature. The infinite uncertainty of outer fate is required, I fear, for profounder lovers to become fully conscious of inner certainty. We express this often in the familiar phrase: Lovers must know heartbreak in their love before it is secure.

The most necessary insight, however, that such tragic love can bring to participants and observers alike is that it has its being beyond the physiological and psychological, that it is indeed a cosmic force. When we see lovers assert the unity of their being in the face of desolation and destruction, a being in the midst of, but also above, conflict, we are forced to acknowledge the transcendent character of love. The lovers exemplify it, they do not create it; they are caught up in it rather than possess it. Love's very nature is to be ecstatic, to draw single units out of themselves and into a higher unity. Its roots are in the widest reaches of being itself, uniting the human entity to the rest of creation. When we confront a love of this tragic kind, we are nearly forced to say, foolishly wise: This is the way the world is. Though we may forget tomorrow what it teaches us today, we are dimly aware that other dimensions of reality exist than are disclosed to everyday moods.

That such love is inexorably wedded to war, we may justly doubt, but that war has often enabled lovers to understand the true fount and origin of their love is also beyond dispute. It is, of all the forms of erotic love, the least wedded to violence. Clearly, the reason is that it is the most integral, uniting, as it does, not only two individuals to each other, but two individuals to the wider realms of being. That even this does not always bring them peace is an indication that the world substance itself, whatever it may be, is not harmonious, complete, or single. True lovers hate war with all their heart, since it demonstrates too well that others have not found the secret of life that they know. But perhaps even they may sometimes admit that they learned the secret only when suspended over the abyss of death. We human beings are not very creative, otherwise we should have discovered other extreme situations that could serve better than war to teach us what we need to know, and without war's loss and unintelligibility.

It is my belief that there is no higher form of love than this

total involvement of a man and a woman in each other. No
other kind can grant us deeper glimpses into the nature of
man or the world he inhabits. Christian love or Greek friendship, so often declared superior, are simply different, but not
more limitless or rewarding. That this is a faith for which I
cannot adduce evidence, I freely confess. My reason for holding it is simply the belief that no love has a deeper base in
nature or, perhaps, a higher reach in the spirit. Its blindness
to values that other loves know how to cherish is a limitation
to which all forces in human life are subject. The Greeks were
surely wise to deify Aphrodite and to make Eros a child of
her union with Ares.

The threat to life and limb and to all man-created things in
time of war calls up in some men a sentiment of love not closely
related to the erotic, but extending beyond the human sphere.
It might best be designated as an impersonal passion to preserve and succor that which is threatened, or to hold back
from annihilation as much life and material as possible. This
love is protective and maternal in kind. Its nature is perhaps
best expressed in the old English word "concern." What men
are concerned about, as the derivation of the word makes
clear, they are implicated in and related to. The urge to preserve from destruction sometimes takes on comical and even
absurd aspects. But its presence is deeply reassuring, for it
helps to humanize partly the most ferocious battles and to
rescue many spirits for the peace that always follows combat.
If we do not find it in many men as a dominant motive of
character, I think love as concern is widely distributed, and is
discoverable frequently in the least likely prospects. Yes,
soldier-killers, intent upon the inverted creativeness of destruc-

tion, have been known to show more than traces of such love in moments and on occasion.

What is it that men are concerned to preserve and to care for in battle? The most obvious answer is self-preservation, taking care of their own lives. This is true in a different sense from the common biological teaching of self-preservation as a basic instinct that men share with other animals. It is also true in a different sense from the egoistic psychology that traces all motivation to self-interest. He who has seen men throw away their lives in battle when caught up in communal passion or expose themselves recklessly and carelessly to mortal danger will be cured forever of such easy interpretations of human motivation. Nothing is clearer than that men can act contrary to the alleged basic instinct of self-preservation and against all motives of self-interest and egoism. Were it not so, the history of warfare in our civilization would be completely different from what it has been.

Nevertheless, self-preservation is a dependable and pervasive feature of human existence in a deeper sense than egoistic theories suppose. The philosopher Spinoza called it the striving to persevere in our own being, and the phrase is exact. Though striving to persevere in our own being is not absolute (for men may deliberately choose suicide) and not merely biological selfishness (since men are capable of dying for others), it is a power that lies both in and beyond the conscious, rational life. Many a soldier has been surprised to discover the desire to continue in being as a final hold and support, after superhuman exertion and mental strain had robbed him of conscious will, and any religious faith he may have possessed had ceased to be meaningful. The literature of war is full of the accounts of armies, beaten and bled, starved and weakened, yet tenaciously staying alive and rescuing a remnant of their strength and numbers. The account of the ancient Greek Xenophon in the *Anabasis* may be taken as a classic example of this survival power in soldiers. Hardly a major war since Xenophon's time has been without similar feats of endurance, though few have had a chronicler such as he.

What is the relation of possessions to this self-preservative love? Can men in extreme peril separate the rescue of their naked lives from the preservation of their nearest possessions? Possessions are for the combat soldier his only assurance of protection against a threatening world. He cares for them, often with more attention than he pays to his own body. His weapons are in this category, and also some articles of dress and precious souvenirs. The intimate relation of the soldier to his weapons involves more than any love of possessions. Often the vehicles and implements of war come to be a replacement for home. This appears to be the crucial relation of possessions to the impulse of self-preservation. Such possessions are not only an extension of the soldier's own power, but they are his link with past and future. In one of the letters in the volume *Letzte Briefe aus Stalingrad,* we read of a hardened German tank soldier sobbing irresistibly because his tank had been destroyed. Its loss meant more to him than did the loss of his comrades. Why? I think it was because the tank had become an imaginative equivalent of the home he had left. It was a second skin, a protective layer against the harsh outer world.

Modern uniforms are so thin and penetrable. Unlike the heavy mail of earlier times, they offer little protection for body or spirit. Therefore, soldiers tend to hug to themselves several layers of possessions as a symbolic protection and, at the same time, as a link with past security and future hopes.

81

Much of the American soldier's passion for souvenirs in recent wars may have stemmed not so much from a primitive desire to loot or even from the desire to establish in postwar memory his claim "to having been there," though both these motives were undoubtedly present in some degree. Primarily, souvenirs appeared to give the soldier some assurance of his future beyond the destructive environment of the present. They represented a promise that he might survive. They protected him from the feeling of being unbearably exposed and vulnerable, and, so, prevented him from being reduced to his naked life. Perhaps all of us, in peace or in war, use possessions for a similar purpose, as a defense against the world.

In cases of extreme exposure, nevertheless, the majority of soldiers seem able to grasp the difference between life and possessions, and will commonly sacrifice all they have to preserve their own being. As prisoners of war, or on long forced marches, or in campaigns of extreme hazard, soldiers learn more often than civilians ever do that everything external is replaceable, while life is not. When a soldier has had to face death often enough, something like a rough hierarchy of values develops in even the simplest mind, and life is nearly always ahead of possessions in the scale. Selfish, egotistical natures prove in such situations to possess less of the genuine love of self-preservation than do others who on the surface are not so eager for life. I suppose the shallow nature is not easily able to view his naked existence, since part of his being is having. Hence soldiers like this often lose their lives in the effort to hold on to some treasured possession.

One would think that learning to do without possessions, experiencing the loss of external holdings, might produce a peculiar blessing for the soldier in his future life as a civilian. But in fact most soldiers quickly forget their wartime order of values when they return to the security of peace, as most of us forget the blessings of health when we are no longer ill. Property comes to be once more an inseparable part of the drive to persevere in our own being. Pure awareness of the struggle to preserve ourselves is not granted to us often in life, just as the imminence of death at any moment of our lives is commonly concealed from us by unconscious suppression.

Preservative love, or concern, is clearly observed in combat in a soldier's care for life other than his own. There is something endlessly instructive in the spectacle of doctors and nurses fighting stubbornly to preserve life and minimal health amid chaos. And the medical corpsman whose duty it is to recover the wounded from front lines often overcomes his fear of death and frightful weariness in performing his work. Sympathy and tenderheartedness are not notably present in such people; they quickly grow calloused to suffering. The motive that drives them forward, more than any other, I believe, is an impersonal passion for protecting and conserving life itself.

This impulse is not restricted at all to those whose official duty it is to preserve; it sometimes becomes a general passion and finds a place in the majority of soldiers. Waifs and orphans and lost pets have a peculiar claim on the affections of combat soldiers, who lavish upon them unusual care and tenderness. For the most part, there is little affinity between protector and protected in these cases. The soldiers are moved by the impersonal compassion that the fragility and helplessness of mortal creatures can call up in most of us. This frequently extends to the enemy wounded. Medical men will risk their lives on occasion to rescue wounded enemy soldiers, and doctors in field hospitals will fight as obstinately for the one as the other. The distinction between friend and foe has here been erased by the recognition of the helplessness of a creature whose life is threatened with extinction.

Superficially, this concern for preserving life other than one's own appears to be separated by a deep gulf from the instinct for self-preservation. The one begins, many will say, only when the other is assured. Yet this is not so. Often on the battlefield the desire to persevere in our being and the preservation of other life are seen to be closely related below the conscious level. The thousand anonymous acts of concern for the life that is exposed to shot and shell is testimony to an ultimate unity between these impulses.

Among the many examples in war literature of concern for preserving others, two in particular have a haunting quality in my memory. In Stephen Crane's *The Red Badge of Courage*, the young soldier who is the focus of the story has fled the battlefield in panic and is wandering around lost and nearly demented somewhere in the immediate rear of the confused struggle. Then an older soldier, a simple man who is an island of gentleness, aids him through the falling darkness back to his regiment and company, where he regains his bearings and courage once again. The act is a wholly gratuitous one. The young soldier does not even see the face of his anonymous savior, much less have the presence of mind to thank him. And the old soldier, for his part, has no thought of doing anything deserving of praise. His was not so much an act of choice as an act of unconscious preservation without much specific feeling on his part for the youth. Though Crane has dealt with fictional characters in this remarkable story, there are thousands of soldiers who will testify to the authenticity of such incidents in combat.

In Tolstoi's *War and Peace*, it is the wealthy and cultured Pierre who is kept in possession of his physical and moral powers by the childlike peasant Karatiev during the period both are prisoners of the French in Moscow and later on the nightmarish retreat with the disorganized army of Napoleon. The contrast between these two men could hardly be greater, yet Pierre becomes aware of how infinitely preservative, and even redeeming, the concern of this simple man for another's life and well-being can be. For Karatiev, taking care of Pierre is not greatly different from taking care of the animals on his father's farm, or, indeed, taking care of plants and the good earth. His instincts are all directed toward countering the threat of annihilation that surrounds life everywhere.

If we ask about the nature of love as concern, I think we can discover some characteristic features that make it different from other forms of love. Unlike the highest type of erotic love, it is directed to general goals and is of communal, more than individual, character. Whether the concern is for one's own being and chances of survival or whether it is directed to the preservation of other life, I doubt if its nature is altered. The object of one's care is less essential than the presence of the need to take care and to preserve. The characteristic mood that accompanies love as concern is neither deep joy nor unrestrained grief, so often typical of erotic love. Concerned love knows relief and it knows anxiety in its depths, but seldom does it put everything at stake on the preservation of this or that life or treasure. Its care is for the whole and not the part.

This love is, in men, evidently pervasive and immanent rather than ecstatic. It does not seize us from without, but arises out of our own nature. Hence it may be less periodic and more dependable than erotic love, though less able to dominate many men in moments of crisis. After we have raged through wars that lasted years, we have always had to make

peace again. Then we are dependent upon this desire, which
has long been subordinated in us by war, to cultivate and
reconstruct. Were this impulse not pervasive and dependable,
the race of man would hardly have survived and grown so
powerful on this planet, surrounded as we are by manifold
dangers of nature and torn by murderous lusts within our own
species.

I think it is concerned love that, more than anything else,
helps us find our way back to peace again and heals the
hatred of belligerents for each other. When soldiers lose this
need to preserve and become impersonal killers, they are truly
figures of terror. Fortunately, few men ever obliterate this
kind of love altogether, though they may well become indifferent to their own fate and full of hatred for a large segment
of mankind. Few of us reflect enough on the good fortune
that attends us as human beings in being pervaded by preservative love. If our wars were to make killers of all combat
soldiers, rather than men who have killed, civilian life would
be endangered for generations or, in fact, made impossible.

Concern in its farther reaches is directed beyond human
life to the works of man and to the things of nature. It is
present in the builder of dwellings and the tiller of the soil as
well as in the thousand modifications of these basic occupa-
tions. We see it, if we have thoughtful eyes, at work everywhere, and the slightest incident in war can teach us more about
it than the longest campaign. I remember riding through Germany in the last days of World War II, in pursuit of the disorganized enemy. Outside a battered city somewhere in Württemberg there was a lovely terraced plot of ground on which a
house had stood. It had been razed by bombs and fire, and
even the fence around it had been destroyed. Only the front
gate remained, though it was awry on its hinges and partly

smashed. As my jeep passed, I caught a glimpse of the owner carefully working to repair the gate. The sight struck me at first as absurd and comical in the extreme, for the gate opened on nothing any longer. But the recollection was deeply cheering, and much later I realized why. The repair of the gate symbolized perfectly the civilizing impulse in human creatures, our urge to preserve and conserve, to take care and to cultivate.

Today many are astonished by the way Germans, for example, rebuild their shattered cities with houses meant to last for a century, when they can hardly be sure that the uneasy peace will endure for five years. Such observers may conclude that Germans are incurably optimistic. In fact, of course, they are not. They themselves scarcely know why they work so hard and build so permanently when they lie under the shadow of the iron curtain. Realistically seen, they are probably foolish. But, after a period of destructive lust, such permanent building satisfies a deep impulse in this people to give full play to conservative and constructive powers. One might think that after three decades or more of extreme disorder and conflict, these powers would be paralyzed, or at least lamed. Yet whatever else has been lost in the German nation, and much has been lost, resistance to destruction and to chaos is still strong. No modern war has until now lasted long enough to contract this preservative love to mere survival of the individual naked life or to make men in large numbers unregenerate killers. Such wars are possible in the future. But the civilizing impulse is strong indeed, and frequently carries us along after reason and will have been temporarily overpowered.

Pervasive as this love is, and connected with the very structure of civilization, its appeal is always greatest when destruction is close at hand and threatening to overwhelm us. I cannot believe that wars are necessary for the fulfillment of this form of love, but it does get called into play most prominently in periods of calamity and raging wars. The delight in destruction is its complete antagonist; therefore, we ought not to be surprised that love as concern is most impressive in time of conflict. It was very important to me.

Perhaps it is this inactivity of the past few days that is affecting me. But Despair is clutching at me often of late, particularly as I lie in bed at night. I need to believe more. I need faith in love and in God. I guess I need to love more. . . . I want so much to come out of it a chastened and wiser person, so that I may be something to others in the postwar world. I need to overcome my gloomy and foreboding spirit.

Again, as in the highest form of erotic love, this kind of love produces a kind of awareness that is lacking in normal life. Our deeper powers lie dormant and undeveloped unless we are pushed to the abyss. Perhaps those philosophers of history are right who read civilization in terms of alternating periods of conservation and destruction, and hold that both are necessary for any real progress. For them, the delight in destruction and preservative love are necessary powers in human history, in some manner complementing each other. The exclusive interest in conserving the already existent would lead to stagnation were it not balanced by destructive forces which periodically sweep away ossified forms as a means of renewal. Love as concern for preserving in being is only meaningful, these philosophers would hold, when it is pitted against revolutionary forces of destruction. I do not know. At all events, I have never again in my life been so aware of the beneficent character of concern as during the war years.

There is another kind of love, with no relation to destruction, that men sometimes experience in war in the most crucial way. It is the love we call friendship. Now friendship has often enough been defined in our tradition as that relationship between human beings in which each dispassionately seeks the welfare of the other. Friendship is thus thought to be the most unselfish form of love, since in the pure state it devotes itself without reserve to the interests of the other. Accordingly, many societies have exalted friendship as the noblest of all relationships, and even the founder of Christianity, to whom another form of love took precedence, is declared to have said: "Greater love has no man than this, that a man lay down his life for his friends."

What meaning has friendship for warriors? How can a young man endure battle when the fear of death is doubled, when not only his own life but that of his friend is at stake? Is the quality of this relationship heightened or reduced by the dread strain of war? Before trying to answer these questions, I must first attempt to make clear a basic difference between friends and comrades. Only those men or women can be friends, I believe, who possess an intellectual and emotional affinity for each other. They must be predetermined for each other, as it were, and then must discover each other, something that happens rarely enough in peace or war.

Though many men never have a friend, and even the most fortunate of us can have few, comradeship is fortunately within reach of the vast majority. Suffering and danger cannot create friendship, but they make all the difference in comradeship. Men who have lived through hard and dangerous experiences together are frequently deceived about their relationship. Comrades love one another like brothers, and under the influence of shared experience commonly vow to remain true friends for the rest of their lives. But when other experiences intervene and common memories dim, they gradually become strangers. At veterans' conventions they can usually regain the old feelings only with the aid of alcoholic stimulation. The false heartiness and sentimentality of such encounters are oppressive and pathetic. Men who once knew genuine closeness to each other through hazardous experience have lost one another forever. And since most men rarely attain anything closer to friendship than this, the loss of comradeship cannot be taken lightly. When veterans try to feel for their old buddies what they felt in battle and fail, they frequently cherish somewhere in their secret memories the unsentimental original passion.

The essential difference between comradeship and friendship consists, it seems to me, in a heightened awareness of the self in friendship and in the suppression of self-awareness in comradeship. Friends do not seek to lose their identity, as comrades and erotic lovers do. On the contrary, friends find themselves in each other and thereby gain greater self-knowledge and self-possession. They discover in their own breasts, as a consequence of their friendship, hitherto unknown potentialities for joy and understanding. This fact does not make friendship a higher form of selfishness, as some misguided people have thought, for we do not seek such advantages in friendship for ourselves. Our concern, insofar as we are genuine friends, is for the friend. That we ourselves also benefit so greatly reveals one of the hidden laws of human affinity. While comradeship wants to break down the walls of self, friendship seeks to expand these walls and keep them intact. The one relationship is ecstatic, the other is wholly individual. Most of us are not capable of meeting the demands on self that friendship brings, whereas comradeship is in most respects an easing of these demands. Comrades are content to be what they are and to rest in their emotional bliss. Friends must always explore and probe each other, in the attempt to make each one complete through drawing out the secrets of another's being. Yet each recognizes that the inner fountain of the other is inexhaustible. Friends are not satiable, as comrades so often are when danger is past.

"That a man lay down his life for his friends" is indeed a hard saying and testifies to a supreme act of fortitude. Friends live for each other and possess no desire whatsoever for self-sacrifice. When a man dies for his friend, he does it deliberately and not in an ecstasy of emotion. Dying for one's comrades, on the other hand, is a phenomenon occurring in every war, which can hardly be thought of as an act of superhuman courage. The impulse to self-sacrifice is an intrinsic element in the association of organized men in pursuit of a dangerous and difficult goal.

For friends, however, dying is terribly hard, even for each other; both have so much to lose. The natural fear of dying is not so hard for them to overcome. What is hard is the loss or diminution of companionship through death. Friends know —I am tempted to say, only friends know—what they are giving up through self-sacrifice. It is said, to be sure, that they can communicate with one another even beyond death, but the loss is nevertheless cruel and final. Too often at moments of greatest need, when one's friend is dead, communication is broken off and one's dialogue becomes monologue. Friends can hardly escape the recognition of death as unmitigated evil and the most formidable opponent of their highest value.

War and battle create for this love both a peculiar kind of security and a kind of exposure, which other forms of love seldom know. The security arises from the insulation that friendship affords against the hatreds and the hopelessness that combat often brings. Even though one friend may be in safety at home, the friend who fights knows that somewhere the other is participating in his life. Through letters he can communicate his deepest feelings and his explorations of the evil experiences through which he is passing. Even when letters are cut off, friends can communicate in their memories of each other, each explaining in imagination to the other and having the assurance of being understood. There is joy in having a person who understands completely and whom you understand. It insulates the soldier's heart without closing his mind to the experiences he is undergoing. The German poet Goethe put nearly perfectly the situation of friends even in wartime. The English translation is by J. S. Dwight.

> *Selig, wer sich vor der Welt*
> *Ohne Hass verschliesst,*
> *Einen Freund am Busen hält*
> *Und mit dem geniesst,*
>
> *Was, von Menschen nicht gewusst*
> *Oder nicht bedacht,*
> *Durch das Labyrinth der Brust*
> *Wandelt in der Nacht.*

> Happy he who, hating none,
> Leaves the world's dull noise,
> And with trusty friend alone,
> Quietly enjoys
>
> What, forever unexpressed,
> Hid from common sight,
> Through the mazes of the breast
> Softly steals by night!

Friends can indeed close themselves without hatred from the world and draw from the labyrinth of each other's being inexhaustible wealth. They can thus endure much of war's horror without losing the zest for life. More than that, they can discover meaning in experiences of the most gruesome sort which others do not see. Friendship opens up the world to us by insulating us against passions that narrow our sympathies. It gives us an assurance that we belong in the world and helps to prevent the sense of strangeness and lostness that afflicts sensitive people in an atmosphere of hatred and destruction. When we have a friend, we do not feel so much accidents of creation, impotent and foredoomed. The assurance of friendship has been enough to help soldiers over many dreadful things without harm to their integrity.

But friendship makes life doubly dear, and war is always a harvest of death. Hence friends are exposed to an anxiety even greater than that of other lovers. There is no destructive dynamic in friendship, no love of death or sacrifice. Because friends supplement each other, they cannot face the prospect of the other's death without shuddering. Comforts can be easily abjured, dangers easily borne, if death is not the issue. The unendurable fear that grips friends on the battlefield is at the farthest remove from the recklessness of the soldier-killer. Among friends war's ultimate horror is experienced without much counterbalancing compensation. Like love as concern, it is directed toward preservation of being.

In every slain man on the battlefield, one can recognize a possible friend of someone. His fate makes all too clear the horrible arbitrariness of the violence to which my friend is exposed. Therefore, in love as friendship we have the most dependable enemy of war. The possible peaks of intensity and earlier maturity which war may bring to friendship are as nothing compared with the threats of loss it holds. The feelings and the affinities that are the core of friendship are the true

93

opposites of the hostile disposition that underlies all warfare. That the one disposition can so easily destroy the other tempts every man who knows friendship to despair and hopelessness.

When death comes to one's friend in the natural course, his loss is cruel enough, reducing the possibility of comprehending events. But friends in time can grow resigned to the finitude of existence, and old age, with its infirmities, helps to reconcile most of us to death. Friendship cut off in its flower by war's arbitrariness is likely to seem the height of unreason and madness. What earlier had been luminous, ordered, and purposeful in experience becomes suddenly emptied of meaning. Unlike other loves, the preciousness of friendship has no connection with its precariousness. Hence no ultimate consolation is possible for the loss of a friend. Love as concern can find new being to preserve and care for; its affection is not individualized. Erotic love can usually, though not always, find itself renewed when time has passed. The companionship of a lost friend is not replaceable.

I do not mean to assert that erotic love, in which the whole person is involved, and love as concern for preservation are less inimical to war than is love as friendship. Analysis of the distinctive forms of love should not betray us into forgetting their blood relationship. These three forms alike stand to lose in battle what makes life dear to them. Love in all three forms stands clearly in opposition to Ares and carries the hope of ultimate freedom from his reign. We do well to remember that love is a genus with many species, and there is little danger of exhausting the inner relations of the species. Those psychologists who find erotic elements in friendship and in maternal love are hardly wrong. And I have intimated already that there is a close affinity between love as concern and love as friendship.

What has become clear to me, however, as I have meditated on love and war, is that battle offers a very different exercise field for these different forms of love. Insofar as Eros is physical passion and sensual impulsion, war has been from of old its true mate and bedfellow, as the ancient myth makes clear. And erotic love of the fuller sort can find a dwelling place in the violence of war that forever astounds us and remains inexplicable. Here Ares and Aphrodite meet as opposites who have a powerful attraction for each other. Love as concern can achieve at times its greatest satisfaction and triumph in struggling to preserve what Ares is intent on destroying. Though deeply opposed to conflict, this love is not as exposed or helpless as is friendship. In the exercise of its ancient rights, preservative love sanctifies even the battlefield by its presence and holds men back from being delivered over wholly to the lustful powers of destruction. But love as friendship, despite its insulation, must subsist haphazardly and as best it may in the midst of war. Its true domain is peace, only peace.

FOUR

THE
SOLDIER'S
RELATIONS
TO DEATH

At the end of the Division area we came upon a recent American cemetery. One hundred and ninety Americans and a few dozen Germans were interred there in plain temporary graves, marked with simple wooden crosses on which were tacked one of their dog tags and a bronze plate with their names, service numbers, ranks, units, and date of death. . . . Officers and privates lay side by side, distinctions of rank being abolished here. The plot was neat and enclosed by a wire fence. . . . It was a cloudy, rain-soaked day, with a chilling breeze. . . . Somehow I had never believed in the reality of war's destructiveness until then. (War journal, February 11, 1944)

When I was in France during the war, I met and lived with a young Parisian brain surgeon, a rare and wonderful and generous person, whose favorite expression was: "Everything

I have, I give away." I never wrote in my journal—I did not have the heart to write—about the last of my visits to him. On this occasion he had received me with the warmth only those know who have long had to associate with people who cannot reach the most cherished areas of the self. But then he launched into an account of a scene he had just witnessed, an execution by the local FFI of a captured Mongolian soldier who had been a member of a German repression unit in the area. Eager to tell me his impressions of the blindfolding and the shooting, the behavior of participants and spectators, he did not notice my dismay. Had he struck me with his fist instead of embracing me, as he had a moment before, I could not have been so dumbfounded and suddenly sick at heart.

How could this sensitive, high-principled man, for whom I had felt an affinity of the deepest kind, attend of his own free will, without hatred, the slaughter of a fellow human being? Often enough he had assured me of his loathing for cruelty and his refusal to participate in the hatreds that consumed the young people associated with him in the Resistance. Even at this moment I knew he was incapable of destroying life. Why would he attend such a spectacle, and why would he want to talk about it?

For a while I did not dare ask him because of the coldness that came over me. Then, since his friendship was dear, I was able to resist the impulse to return to my jeep and drive away and was able to speak of my abhorrence of his deed. We talked at length about the subject of death and of dying. He was convinced that the Mongolian had no thoughts at all about what was happening to him. He had died as an animal does. For this reason, he had been able to view the scene with detachment. I was not so sure. Though the incident remained a barrier between us, which I was not able to overcome, the night's conversation made me think about the elementary facts of facing death, as I had not hitherto done. On the way back to my unit the following day, I began to ponder the question how men at war consider the possibility of their own imminent death. What relations to death can warriors attain, or can they gain any relation to death at all?

In the months that followed, however, I was influenced more than I cared to admit by the regnant mood of recklessness with human life. Men are expendable, as the current phrase had it; life was a commodity to be doled out and used up by a superpersonal will. Probably few of us consciously reorganized our values owing to this fact, but even the simplest mind among us could sense that it mattered relatively little to the collective body whether he survived or not. Though we could not comprehend why death struck others and not us, we learned to accept it as a brute fact. As long as it did not strike one's friends, there was the great temptation to react to it no differently than one did to other occurrences. The dead began to seem both unreal and yet commonplace:

We are now at Artena, very near the front, and are in some danger from artillery fire. This morning when we came up over a fearfully dusty road, we entered Artena far enough to see a dead American soldier over whom flies were swarming. The town is still under shellfire, and there are some twelve dead in the streets. We withdrew to a house on the edge of the town, where I am writing this now. . . . Small cemeteries, hastily constructed, line the road and are everywhere. The roads are a churning mass of traffic and dust, dangerous, unpleasant, necessary—the very substance of war.

The gloomy October air is rent by the roar of big guns. They are not frightening after the first startled awakening. But then one hears the whistle and the rending explosion. . . . I am less fright-

ened than most of the others, I know not why. Eventually one becomes more or less used to it all, if not indifferent.

The shock administered by my friend was enough eventually to arouse me from this collective torpor. From then on I became intensely curious to discover how soldiers react to this absolute, death, in human existence, particularly when they are alone in foxholes without the comfort of comrades. It is not difficult to understand, as I have already pointed out, that communal ecstasy can lead men to forget death and seek immortality in pursuit of shared goals. But ecstasy of any sort is essentially periodic and transient; it cannot be long sustained. How then could youths who had hardly yet begun to live endure the prospect of their own probable death? The fact that thousands of them could do it was palpable enough; the how of doing it was something of a mystery.

One might argue that death in war is merely a matter of increased probability, not different in principle from death in time of peace. But this would be a superficial view, for not the frequency of death but the manner of dying makes a qualitative difference. Death in war is commonly caused by members of my own species actively seeking my end, despite the fact that they may never have seen me and have no personal reason for mortal enmity. It is death brought about by hostile intent rather than by accident or natural causes that separates war from peace so completely. And the fact that death's chief victims in war are young men or youths who are just becoming men contributes greatly to the general mood. For the most part, these youths must take leave of their lives under conditions of exposure, away from home, without the possibility of the dignity and ceremony that help to moderate death's shocking character. The difference is not only between dying and

100

getting killed. It is much more the difference between dying by disease or accident among people who know and cherish you and having your life cut off without preparation by someone who cares not at all for the anguish he causes. This creates the terrible hatred of war, particularly among civilian populations.

The majority of soldiers in modern wars, I am convinced, are able to gain only a negative relation to death. For them, death is a state and a condition so foreign and unreal as to be incomprehensible. They reject it with aversion without bringing its reality to the level of consciousness. Thus, in the summer of 1944, when I was waiting for the invasion of southern France to begin, an invasion I was to join, I wrote:

What do I think of this new adventure looming before me? Today I have thought about it for the first time. It will be dangerous, that is certain. It will also be difficult. But somehow I am unable to anticipate. I simply await—and dream of the end of the war. I daydream more than I used to.

In peacetime, young people are likely to dismiss the fact of death as something that happens to somebody else; seldom do they take seriously the certainty that they themselves will have to cope with it. In war soldiers cannot ignore death, for it is all too prevalent. But imagining what it is like to be dead is endlessly difficult. Imagination and intellect must be operative if we are to bridge the gap between life and death, and many soldiers understandably try to avoid exercising either. Battlefield dead are so passive, and life is, to our Western youth at least, bound up totally with activity and action. Soldiers fall and die in such contorted and unnatural positions, as a rule, that even their comrades find it hard to believe that, shortly before, they were alive. This is part of the mystery of death:

101

those who enter its realm are quickly far removed from the living. In battle, where the demands of action are insistent, the process is, if possible, even more speeded up.

This morning we got word early that we had been selected as the group to enter Rome. . . . Everywhere was the picture of an Army pursuing another, ruined tanks and vehicles of all sorts, houses burned, everything hastily done. The sight of the dead soldiers did not trouble me as much as I had expected. They seemed almost part of the general wreckage, and one found it hard to believe that they had ever been alive, much less a few hours ago.

In mortal danger, numerous soldiers enter into a dazed condition in which all sharpness of consciousness is lost. When in this state, they can be caught up into the fire of communal ecstasy and forget about death by losing their individuality, or they can function like cells in a military organism, doing what is expected of them because it has become automatic. It is astonishing how much of the business of warfare can still be carried on by men who act as automatons, behaving almost as mechanically as the machines they operate.

Most of us remember with a shudder those endless pictures of Hitler's troops, before World War II, riding into one conquered country after another. They were frightening because they not only looked identical in clothing and equipment, but the set expression on their faces appeared to be vacant and purposeless. All humanity had eroded from those faces, so it seemed, and we were confronted by deadly efficient robots who were controlled by a powerful, inhuman will. So it often is in combat itself. Death comes to thousands who are only minimally conscious and snatches them away from life without their awareness of the moment or its significance.

There are two things that promote this drugged state so common in combat: training and fatigue. The routine of military life, the repetition, drill, and uniformity of response, works to dampen and dull any individual intensity of awareness. Even the civilian soldier who finds the military way quite alien and strange can learn to hold fast to the few simple rules, to be a proper cog in the vast machine, and to suspend thoughts that might unfit him for his appointed mission. He learns to expect orders from above and to pass them along to those under his control. Thinking tends to become not only painful but more and more unnecessary.

To be sure, battle often presents the soldier with novelty, demanding initiative, for which he has been unprepared. But this, too, distracts him from thought of death. He is much too busy trying to fit the novel situation into the well-worn patterns of response he has been practicing for many months or years. What does his commander expect of him in this unprecedented situation? Should he advance, stay where he is, or retreat? His mind becomes so preoccupied with the mechanics of action that larger issues never enter, and self-awareness is dimmed to the vanishing point. This is as true of the general as it is of the private soldier, perhaps more true of the general, to whom the battle must conform to some pattern of his long training in strategy and tactics. A psychologist would probably insist that this absorption with routine and details was the mind's escape from its fear of extinction. If so, the escape is usually effective.

The second hindrance to realization of death's imminence is the physical weariness that is usually precedent to any engagement in battle. Loss of sleep, long marches, cold food, and the nervous tension that the destruction common to forward areas evokes combine to exhaust the combat soldier. This weariness can go beyond borders that most of us ever know at other periods in our lives. It alone can so stupefy the senses that soldiers behave like sleepwalkers. Continued over a period of time, such exhaustion can induce men to welcome death as a rest and a change from what they have been doing. I wrote in my journal of my own feeling after hard, bitter months:

The days pass and I become duller of mind and tireder of the war. The way is long and sometimes I question the wisdom of it all, of continuing to live. There may be a real purpose in it all, which is perceived only at the end of the journey. Somehow I feel that is true.

This is part of the unromantic answer to the question how young men can face nearly certain death in war. It comes as a relief from what they are doing. Death appears to be rest; it is quiet, sleep, and even the most stupefied can gain some appreciation of what that means.

I have seen exhausted soldiers sleeping while exposed to the greatest danger of death. It might be said that these soldiers had won some positive relationship to death in conceiving it as sleep and rest. But in most cases, I think, this would be going too far. Men overcome by weariness are not really relating death to rest or sleep; they have simply an overwhelming feeling that change is a necessity and death is a change. Their aversion to the incomprehensible state of death has not been altered, as a few hours' rest makes clear. It has only been superseded by physical need of the most insistent kind.

Yet these explanations do not account completely for the large percentage of soldiers who die in war without being able to face death or gain any relationship to it save one of horror and aversion. The dazed consciousness must have

104

other sources as well. In part it is also due, I believe, to the fear of pain and mutilation which bullets and shrapnel can bring. Pain is something very real in the memories of everyone, as death is not, and most combat soldiers have witnessed enough gaping wounds and listened to the agonized cries of the wounded often enough so that they cannot consciously endure the thought of the same thing happening to them. Though the dread of death may be at the bottom of conscious processes at such moments, the fear of being painfully injured is much in the foreground. This fear dulls self-awareness as effectively as fatigue and routine can and has a more lasting influence. Fear can prey on the mind to the point where it makes a soldier unfit for combat. Usually it rises just high enough to prevent reason, and with it the detachment of self-consciousness, from governing.

Above all, this stupefaction of consciousness is doubtless a function of the total environment of war. To some extent it afflicts everyone much of the time. After a few months in the combat zone, I, at least, found it hard indeed to believe in any other reality than war or to contrast it with any other state.

Sometimes I am overcome with the desire to go off by myself and live in a hermitage. I cannot face the prospect of going back to any of my old haunts after the war. I shall not want to speak of these war years, and I cannot be as I was. What is left?

One does not want to die and cannot live as he would.

The past had grown so distant and unreal that another way of life was hard to imagine. The realization of oneself and the objective conditions of one's life can come in wartime with piercing intensity and unforgettable clarity. But the environment of violence and hatred commonly insulates us against revelations of ourselves by making any break-through to consciousness doubly difficult.

If the majority of soldiers gain no positive relationship to death, there are others who do, and the relationships are of numerous kinds, from the more abstract and conventional to the concrete and personal. There is a type of soldier who considers death very real for others but without power over him. These soldiers cherish the conviction that they are mysteriously impervious to spattering bullets and exploding shells. The little spot of ground on which they stand is rendered secure by their standing on it. Death is an impersonal force that can rob other men of their motion and their powers, but for them it has no body or substance at all. Some soldiers even manage to get through a long war with this conviction unimpaired. It is a conviction that is responsible for much rashness in battle, misnamed courage. Since such soldiers are freed from anxiety, they are frequently able to see the ridiculous and amusing aspects of combat life and provide much priceless cheer and humor for their comrades.

Fortunate is the unit that can count one or more of these soldiers in its ranks; and in fact most units do appear to contain them. They are a perennial phenomenon in war, a cause of wonder and admiration, as though their like had never been. Sometimes they become the subject of war tales, which quickly take on mythlike proportions. If such soldiers command men, as frequently happens, they have the capacity to inspire their troops to deeds of recklessness and self-sacrifice.

In most of these soldiers, the source of their relationship toward death—as a reality for others only—is not too difficult to discover. They have simply preserved their childish illusion that they are the center of the world and are therefore

106

immortal. Their ego is incredibly naïve and their self-confidence absurd to anyone who is capable of regarding them coldly. Civilian life contains many such naïve egoists, I am convinced, but the presence of danger and the seemingly arbitrary fortunes of war weaken the illusion of indestructibility in most delayed adolescents. In others, stronger shocks are required. Until a drastic occurrence touches them closely, they preserve their fantastic faith. Perhaps their own wounding is necessary. The look of shock and outrage on such a soldier's face when that happens is likely to be unforgettable. At one cruel stroke he loses forever the faith in his physical immortality. His psychological adjustment to the new world he has to inhabit is certain to be harder than the physical recovery from his wounds. Most of us learn when we are younger, at home and gradually, to accept the sad truth that the world does not revolve around us. Even then the discovery is not easy or simple. At the front or in a field hospital, this truth is disillusioning in the extreme. The soldier who learns it there will never be the same again. Sometimes he becomes a cynic, his former humor and lightheartedness utterly corroded by a lost trust in the world he inhabits. He may also become a coward, with blanching fear of all danger, a man henceforth useless to his military unit.

When the belief in one's indestructibility is due to a defect of imagination, other experiences than being wounded may suffice to waken the soldier to his situation. It may be the death of an acquaintance in his arms, where the transition between life and death is made imaginatively visible for the first time, or it may be the rare sight of death in lifelike form that startles him into self-consciousness. Animals on the battlefield sometimes afford the most memorable examples of the latter.

Those American soldiers who came up Route Six in Italy

on the way to Rome on April 4 or 5, 1944, will scarcely have forgotten the magnificent horses that were shot down, apparently by our fliers, as they were fleeing madly northward. The retreating Germans had run out of fuel for their vehicles and must have commandeered the horses from the estate of some wealthy fancier of such creatures. The horses had fallen in harness, with their heads high in the air, eyes opened and distended in terror. Their legs had folded under them, as though paralyzed, and they lay upright on their bellies, looking as if they wanted to continue their flight without means of locomotion. There were many of them, in columns, and the strafing bullet wounds were hardly visible. The dead soldiers who lay around, German and American, in the usual distorted postures, could not persuade us that they had been alive a few hours before, but hardly anyone was able to look at the horses without a shudder. Little imagination was required to see what death was like, for the eyes of those thoroughbred animals contained its image in painful clarity. Such scenes, repeated on different battlefields and in every war, often suffice to imprint on the minds of some soldiers the indelible truth that death plays no favorites. I learned this truth.

This morning we went to Laiatico, a town that had been shelled to pieces by German artillery in the past two days and presented as grim an aspect as any we have yet seen. A huge dead horse was lying inside one of the ruined houses, and the smell of death was everywhere. At first there was no sight of civilians, but we found them later, collected in shelters, many wounded, all miserable, all frightened because the town was still receiving an occasional shell. . . . In many ways this town was no different from the others, but it left a grimmer impression. It made me realize afresh what war is. . . . The citizenry was bitter. There was much pillaging and theft on the part of civilians, also soldiers, while the populace was

*in air-raid shelters. What a brute man is. He thrives on his fellow's
misery.*

*We are in Laiatico. . . . The smell of death is everywhere. Five
civilians were killed and lay in the bombed-out church for a week
until the smell was unbearable. Yesterday I took a walk to the
outskirts of the village and discovered an American soldier of our
Division lying dead in a potato patch. He had not been dead long.
I could discover no bullet wound, but he had fallen backward
with his head downhill and the blood had run into his face and
filled up his throat and mouth. . . . Looking closer I discovered
that he was very young, a lad from Louisiana, his dog tag revealed. I have forgotten his name. The flies had arrived already
and were feasting on the blood in his open mouth. . . . A little
farther on were the carcasses of four huge oxen, killed by shells.
They, too, presented a horrible sight, with their huge bodies stiff
and their legs in the air. A farmhouse stood nearby, riddled by
shot and shell. The inhabitants had fled. Inside the house a door
banged with the gusts of air. Chickens and a few white rabbits
were around the yard and one live ox stood stoically and uncon-
cerned nearby. . . .*

But in some few men the illusion of indestructibility is occasioned by deeper causes than deficient imagination or delayed adolescence. It is a function of an indomitable will to
power which refuses to recognize ordinary mortality. Such
men have a fanatic faith in their destiny which is only
strengthened by narrow escapes and the sight of death in
manifold forms. They are commonly leaders and win recognition as fearless warriors whose iron nerves and will to victory
are out of all proportion to those of other men. We know these
exceptional persons from the pages of military history, and
perhaps many of us have seen their smaller counterparts in our
own ranks. Nothing but their own death will rob them of their
illusion, and it is one of the mysteries of combat that they so

rarely get killed. Little do they have to recommend them as friends or comrades. As a rule, they are vain and empty, contemptuous of all who are not like themselves. Battle appears to be their very element, and in that element men will not hesitate to pay them homage. Nevertheless, it is not courage they display, not the human will triumphing over fate. If their vitality and their will are admirable in themselves, there is little that is specifically human about their whole mentality. They hardly recognize other men as such and are capable of walking over bodies, living or dead, without a qualm. In their secret hearts they despise friend and foe equally, these supreme egoists. If nature brought many such forth, the world would be more of a shambles after warfare than it customarily is.

For those who have never shared this illusion that death is something that happens only to others, it is probably foolhardy to try to formulate the relation to death this type of soldier sustains. At all events it *is* a relation, something that can hardly be said of the earlier-mentioned and much more common type. For this soldier, death is envisioned as an external power which subjects others to its realm and makes them fearful. The naïve egoist has thus no wish to banish this power. From his fearlessness before it, he gains his distinctiveness. He can control it and deal it out, but into its mysteries he has no wish to penetrate. Perhaps he sometimes wonders why others appear to know more about death than he, though he is normally incurious. His vitality and egoism are in an utterly separate sphere from death, and they, too, are equally taken for granted. There can be no intimacy between these spheres; at most, an empirical recognition on the part of the living that death is real, for it has swallowed up some of "the others." This soldier's mind is clear enough when he thinks of death and his eye is undazed when he views dead bodies, but neither penetrates far. Without communication with each other, life and death remain powers that exist side by side, unfathomed and lacking mystery.

An opposite relation to death is possibly more prevalent among soldiers in modern wars and more understandable to Americans in general, even if scorned. Here death is an intimate and repugnant enemy before whose threat and presence one can only flee in terror. There are soldiers in nearly every unit who can endure every hardship and humiliation of military life without flinching, yet cannot face personal danger with any composure at all. Such soldiers feel that all bullets are intended for them and every shell likely to land on the particular spot they have selected as temporary shelter. Insatiable death lurks everywhere ready to pounce upon them, and every one of his victims they see makes them the more certain they will be the next one. These soldiers are quickly found out in combat and become the butt of their comrades' ridicule and contempt. There is a peculiar derogation in the epithet "coward" in wartime, for war of course glorifies courage above all other virtues. Hence the men who are unable to face the prospect of death without terror are so branded and must endure, at least in military service, insults and contumely of every sort. Few people ask why the coward fears death excessively or seek to understand the complex motives underlying his relation to the world or to death. In inquiring into this relation toward death as one of unreasoning terror on the part of the soldier-coward, I want to emphasize that the term "coward" is used in a more restrictive sense than is commonly done.

It is necessary to distinguish the person who is an occasional coward in the face of death from the constitutional coward. In

111

almost everyone at times, there is a coward lurking. The literature of war is replete with instances of elite troops seized with
panic fear, of the bravest soldiers fleeing in terror at some
time in their career. Cowardice in this sense is, like rashness,
a group phenomenon and greatly contagious. When the individual is caught unprepared, he becomes a victim of the mass
will, which overflows him and sweeps him away. Students of
mass psychology believe they know when and under what
conditions the individual is likely to respond to these mass
emotions. Commanders of troops can never be sure how their
units will respond to the effect of surprise or close-contact
fighting. But the constitutional coward hardly surprises anyone; he simply cannot endure combat when personal danger
becomes acute.

Under peaceful conditions, this excessive fear of death
might remain unknown, even to the coward himself, and after
a war the coward is quite capable of concealing or forgetting
it for the further duration of his life. Cowardice, like courage,
is a complex quality, and it does not follow that an excessive
fear of death always colors all other relations a coward sustains to life. In fact, the coward may be a good citizen, a
considerate husband and father, a successful legionnaire. In
most respects he is likely to be a more pleasing peacetime
companion than the man who believes himself indestructible.

As moral courage is distinguishable from physical courage,
a man being capable of possessing the one without the other,
so physical cowardice is different from moral cowardice. Civilian life seldom gives men opportunity to test their capacity
to face death. Doubtless there are thousands who have no idea
whether they are cowards in the military sense. Only when
they come to their deathbed will their fortitude or lack of it
be revealed to themselves, and even there it may be hidden

because we have learned well how to avoid the issue through the art and science of medicine.

The coward in battle, however, dies a thousand deaths, as the proverb has it, and each one is mentally painful beyond measure. Actually, of course, his physical death is more likely than is that of the courageous soldier, for he cannot remain still. Continually he suffers the illusion that another piece of earth is more secure than the one he presently inhabits. Even his sleep is troubled, since he follows in his unconscious mind the sound of incoming or outgoing shells. The slightest change in direction or distance of firing is sufficient to wake him and cause him to seek a presumably safer spot elsewhere. Most veterans have their own memories of this kind of soldier, but none could be more typical than a companion of mine during the Italian and French campaigns. This handsome youth, of Irish descent, first aroused our merriment because he was so attached to his helmet that he wore it while sleeping, despite the obvious discomfort. When incoming shells exploded anywhere within miles of us, he would pull a table over his sleeping bag or, more often, get up, cursing horribly, and descend to the cellar of the building we were using, no matter how dank, for the remainder of the night. It was his lamentable fate to land on D day in southern France, and our chafing was mixed with pity at what Tom had to suffer in prospect. Fortunately, his landing craft was not fired upon, and, when our unit was reunited in a chalet a few hundred yards from shore, we found Tom pale yet reasonably composed. Just then, however, a German plane came over and released a bomb which landed squarely, with a terrific explosion, on another craft nearing the shore. There was great destruction, for the boat contained, in addition to soldiers, a lot of ammunition, which exploded at intervals until the boat sank hours later.

Though we were at a safe distance from it, Tom immediately lost his voice. He could not speak above a hoarse whisper for two or three days. In spite of our horror at the carnage on the beach, we were forced to laugh at our companion, who could not refrain from chattering, in a semiaudible croak, the rest of the evening. Not trusting the security of the chalet for sleeping, he carried his sleeping bag into a ravine for the night, and was nearly eaten up by red ants. They were not sufficient, needless to say, to make him return to the luxury of a comfortable bed with the rest of our unit.

What is it that this man possessed or lacked that separates him so sharply from the soldier beside him who could remain reasonably calm in the presence of danger to his life? I think the answer can only be that he lacked, above all else, a sense of union with his fellows. The coward may have comrades, but they are not able to sustain him emotionally. His relation to them is not one of depth or inner community. They are merely part of the external furniture of his life. He is unable to comprehend those who throw away their lives from rashness or joy in sacrifice. Indeed, it is impossible for him to comprehend how other values can equal or surpass the value of his own life. To all arguments concerning duty, honor, or the respect of friends, his retort is sure to be: "What do they matter if I am no longer alive to know about them?" This question is unanswerable, because for the coward it is no question but a dogmatic certainty. The Solomonian wisdom "It is better to be a living dog than a dead lion" exactly fits his conviction.

If the coward does not know the sense of a common effort and a common fate, he has, unfortunately, not gained in its place any strong individuality or any full awareness of self. It is a fact often enough noticed that people who are deficient in the capacity for love hold onto life with the greatest tenacity. The coward's fear of death stems in large part from his incapacity to love anything but his own body with passion. He is an egotist because he does not possess enough self-assurance to be an egoist. The inability to participate in others' lives stands in the way of his developing any inner resources sufficient to overcome the terror of death. His is truly a pitiable figure in combat, for fear and danger drive him more and more into the confines of his own skin and make him more and more into a mindless body.

This soldier's relation to death is a genuine one, and by no means negative. Before the dread and monstrous reality, the coward feels all the frailty and exposure of his existence, and senses that the struggle is an unequal one. Even temporary survival must be procured by careful stratagems and by yielding dignity here and there. Death is a personal enemy of his, a relentless, absolute, all-encompassing enemy. But the coward's inner poverty of life and love makes him no fit antagonist. I think it must be said that his fear is not to be separated from a dim recognition that he belongs to this opponent. In spite of himself, death is not remote from his inner self and all his impulses. The coward, unrelated to his fellows, has an insufficient hold on life and is not in charge of himself or his fate. A brave man might fear death as an opponent possessing all the qualities opposite to those which he himself possesses. His discipline in the face of this enemy is governed by the recognition that death is implacable and will ultimately triumph in an outward sense. But for the coward death is within him. He is related to this most gruesome enemy, and the more he struggles to escape the greater is his captivity. When the coward's body is finally yielded up to death, there is nothing instructive or solemn about the spectacle. Few scenes are more deeply unpleasant.

If the majority of American soldiers find it impossible to attain any other relation to death than that of rejection or negation, we should not hastily conclude that a positive and acceptive relation is evidence of an unnatural or deviant mentality. There are soldiers in the Anglo-Saxon world and perhaps many more in Teutonic and Slavic lands, to say nothing of the Orient, for whom death is a fulfillment. Unless we try to understand the motivation of this kind of soldier, we can make no claim to grasping the full nature of *Homo furens*.

Here again, however, it is impossible to treat the genus and disregard the numerous species. Not all soldiers who find fulfillment in death seek the same kind of fulfillment, and their motivations are frequently very diverse. For some, death is only a *means* to fulfillment. Thus it is, for example, with the soldier who sacrifices his life willingly out of love for his country or for a glorified leader or for an ideal like fascism or communism. Such a soldier can enter into death in self-forgetfulness and treat it merely as an incident in comparison with the reality that fills his being. He uses death as a means by which to prove his love and devotion to something beyond himself. Death is welcomed not for itself, but as a sign of his utter faithfulness. Some leaders can call forth in their men this unbounded eagerness to die for them. The simple soldier who obeys such an impulse to self-sacrifice feels in an irrational way that his leader will be mightily satisfied with him for so doing. Any wrath his leader may nurse at a perverse turn of events will be appeased by this act of selflessness. A soldier like this steps into death, as it were, with his eyes fixed elsewhere. He has not thought much or at all about what

116

it is like to be dead or what dying signifies, because he is overcome by enthusiasm for some living ideal or person sufficient to render his own independent existence of lesser value.

For the deeply religious soldier, on the other hand, death can be a fulfillment in a very different sense from self-sacrifice. If he chances to be a follower of those religions that teach eternal life, then physical death is a portal for him to a greater and immeasurably happier life beyond. Though the numbers of such soldiers have decreased markedly in our century, we should not forget that thousands of them still take part in every major war. I was, in fact, astonished to find how many of the farewell letters written by those condemned for the unsuccessful attempt on Hitler's life in 1944 were pervaded by faith in a life to come. Sometimes this is a minimal faith, a forlorn hope, but there can be little doubt that many soldiers cherish it still. The genuinely otherworldly consciousness, so much scorned as an escape in recent times, is increasingly misunderstood by people who take little time for reflection. Their customary charge that the hope of life after death is camouflaged egotism and vanity applies only to those who attempt to use religious faith rather than to be used by it.

For the soldier who is not a foxhole convert to faith, death is something other than a barrier placed between him and the painless life on the other side. On the contrary, genuine otherworldliness regards death as an enemy only so long as the individual has not discovered his purpose in being alive, for reaching the goal is no simple process of stepping over a dark threshold. Death is, instead, a power on earth to be overcome; it is a last great obstacle and a necessary trial for the pilgrim on life's way. In the end it will prove, of course, to be a veil of illusion to the faithful one, but he must overcome the world to learn this secret. His proper posture will be to meet death face-to-face and gain the assurance that the closer he comes the more peaceful and indeed joyous his journey. If anyone doubts that such people can confront death with serenity and cheer, let him read the communications of true believers condemned to die and awaiting execution. Their one concern is commonly those who are left behind without the calm and peace that they, the condemned, have won.

Perhaps I can state this otherworldly relation to death in more concrete form. Death is a fulfillment, not in the sense of a consummation, but as the final triumph of the spirit over the forces that would hinder it from life everlasting. There are, to be sure, some kinds of otherworldliness that conceive of trials continuing after death, when the soul is in purgatory, but there any aid it receives must be external to it and not something that the soul can itself accomplish. Rather than being a barrier between me and true bliss, death is the path that brings me there when I have learned to tread it. Christian and non-Christian otherworldliness are at one in teaching that life is a process of overcoming the natural and instinctive. A rebirth is required, a change in direction which is radical, to the point where life will not be considered any longer as self-sustaining or self-explanatory, but, rather, as a gift that is redeemable by the giver at any moment under any condition. Those who are born again to the spirit, as the Christian puts it, regard death as that part of life which does not belong to one's essence.

The religious man is constantly dying to those aspects of self and the world that becloud the true eternal existence. Physical death is only the final stage in a long-continued struggle to overcome "the world." In this sense, otherworldliness regards death as a fulfillment of life's mission in this world; death is what the believer has been constantly surpass-

118

ing. When physical death approaches, it is easy to enter into and full of promise. For some it is the final stripping away of the self and its tiny concerns, all that is particular and merely personal. Others regard death as the final purification of the self, freeing it from what remains of all imperfections and blemishes.

Can the otherworldly soldier who is caught up in action and thrown together with violent men preserve his peacetime convictions of death as a final conquest? Or is not this whole conception and mentality peculiar to older and more weary spirits, as many assert? The answer is, I think, that otherworldliness is as likely to flourish among men at war as among men at peace. If there is a difference, it lies in the fact that combat matures men quickly and perhaps particularly in their ways of regarding life and death. There may be more time for thinking and more loneliness in foxholes at the front than in secure homes, and time is measured in other ways than by clocks and calendars. For soldiers who have entered military service with a firm otherworldly faith, there is frequently little difficulty in continuing to regard death as they did before, and the violence all about may well strengthen, rather than weaken, their convictions. On the other hand, soldiers whose religious faith is chiefly this-worldly, that is, social and ethical in content, often find war's destruction wreaking havoc with their belief.

The otherworldly soldier may prudently seek to stay alive as long as the worldly one. Unless he is a fanatic, he tries to listen to inner commands before acting rashly. But the difference becomes apparent when the chances of surviving a given engagement are reduced and death becomes as nearly certain as it ever does in combat. Then such an otherworldly soldier rarely cringes from his fate, does not become de-

119

spondent or bitterly reproachful of others. Inwardly he may be exultant or simply collected. What is coming has been determined by greater and wiser forces than he commands, and he is content to repeat: "Thy will be done" or its equivalent. The destroyers of such soldiers are astounded at how "bravely" they die and are sometimes deeply shaken by it. It seems to be contrary to nature. But the steadfastness of that will which is fixed on a life beyond death can endure the pain of dying and sometimes achieve exaltation in the act.

There is another element that commonly makes death easier for such a soldier. For the otherworldly Christian, at least, there is a contradiction in combat and a fearful moral peril. He is conscious of the pacifistic injunctions of his faith and has not been able, in all likelihood, to make the easy distinctions between destroying life in peace and in war that governments insist upon. Even though he may have privately determined that no one shall fall by his hand, his conscience seldom leaves him in peace. The Biblical dictum that "all who take the sword will perish by the sword" has persuaded him, perhaps, that it is no more than just that he should leave his young life in this unholy war.

This is also particularly true for the soldier whose religious search is not guided by life after death, but is strongly moral. Death can become for him, a participant in what he considers the crime of warfare, a way of atonement, especially appropriate, even if insufficient. Though he cannot greet death joyously, as one expecting a great translation into the eternal, he can greet it calmly and inwardly at peace as the path to a mind at one with itself.

Occasionally on the battlefield one is haunted by the face of a dead soldier on which there is stamped a kind of unearthly serenity. I remember a handsome young German soldier, near the end of World War II, who had been hanged by the SS troops, possibly because he wanted to surrender a few hours earlier than they. His body was swaying in the breeze beneath a tree along the road on which my jeep was traveling. I stopped and cut the rope that held him. As his body fell to the earth, face upward, my gaze was caught and held for some minutes by the expression on his regular features. Seldom have I seen a look of greater inner happiness on a human face, dead or alive. It was hard to understand how he could have maintained such an expression, for his executioners had hardly granted him the mercy of a broken neck. He had no other wound, and everything about his person and uniform was in perfect order.

I could not rid myself of the conviction that, despite his youth and the approaching end of hostilities, he had suffered gladly this death by execution at the hands of his own people. If in this particular case it is a supposition that cannot be confirmed, we do have evidence of other German soldiers who voluntarily escaped torments of conscience in Hitler's war through death brought about by his hired killers. The perceptive among them knew well enough that dying does not erase guilt, but they also knew that it is the most that conscience and religious faith can demand in situations where more appropriate atonement is not available. We need be under no illusions that only enemy nationals sought similar means of atonement, though the number in any army is not great.

Is there not a relationship to death different from either rejection as an abhorred enemy or acceptance as a path to fulfillment or expiation? Is there not a relationship that, though not so common, is closer to representing the essence of the fighting man? I think so, but to characterize it is not easy. This attitude is more concrete and objective, as a rule, less conventional and perhaps less emotional than the ones I have been concerned with thus far. First let me attempt a general statement of this relation to death and then turn to examples, which are in effect subspecies, or different varieties, of the type.

As a consequence of temperament and experience, some soldiers can learn to regard death as an anticipated experience among other experiences, something they plan to accept when the time comes for what it is. They take death into life, as it were, and seek to make it a part of experience, sometimes winning thereby an intimate relationship. Because they respect death as a power and do not fear it as a blind fate, they are able to reckon their chances in warfare with greater calmness than other soldiers. For them, death is as much a self-evident fact as birth, and they regard as foolish the man who refuses to accept the one as the other. Since moral or religious considerations hardly occupy first rank with such soldiers, they are unlikely to choose death as a means or an end to self-improvement or atonement. However, the more imaginative and thoughtful of this type do regard death as that absolute in human existence which gives life its poignancy and intensity. They do not desire to live forever, for they feel that this would be a sacrifice of quality to gain quantity. In philosophical terms, such soldiers are affirming human finiteness and limitation as a morally desirable fact. Just as the bliss of erotic love is conditioned by its transiency, so life is sweet because of the threats of death that envelop it and in the end swallow it up. Men of this sort are usually in love with life and avid for experience of every sort.

Indeed, experience is the word that best stamps a kind of

unity on a diverse group. Their common relation to death is that of regarding it as neither friend nor foe, but as a possibility for a supreme kind of experience. The less reflective members of this group would certainly never describe this relation in deliberate terms like these; on the contrary, they scorn such verbalizing. Action is their element, and their hearts are in the future as it enfolds itself every day. They look out upon the world as adventure and upon themselves as capable of storming all its ramparts. They are not naïve enough to regard themselves as indestructible, and do not even desire to be. What they desire is experience, and the fuller and more intense that experience is, the more content they are. War offers them something that peace cannot: the opportunity to telescope much experience into short compass. If death be the issue, they are normally fatalists by instinct and can accept it more calmly than the prospect of a boring, empty period in their lives.

Perhaps the least complicated of this type is the dashing, reckless soldier whose perennial charm consists in his devil-may-care attitude toward all the solemn rituals of military protocol. All men at war have known one or two such soldiers and doubtless have blessed them in their hearts. Normally, such a carefree youth is not very curious about the end of his life, though keenly aware that living is sweet because life is fragile and ringed by danger. If he did reflect on death, he would doubtless be in accord with the sentiments of Feeble in the Second Part of Shakespeare's *Henry the Fourth:*

By my troth, I care not; a man can die but once; we owe God a death. . . . And let it go which way it will, he that dies this year is quit for the next.

To the otherworldly soldier, a man like this is incomprehensible, explainable only as an unawakened one; to the coward, he is an utter fool; to the soldier who can face mortal danger only in a daze, he is a subject for admiration and puzzlement. It does not occur to many of them that this carelessness about his life stems from overabundance of it. Consequently, he values other things more highly than life, above all, adventure and full experience. If he were careful and circumspect with his life, most of the joy in living would be gone, for guarding the flame is a way of keeping it from full brilliance. When such a soldier acquires a family and civilian responsibilities, he usually loses some of his gaiety and recklessness. Yet death can never be to him what it is to most other soldiers, for without much reflection he has made it a part of life, and his response to it will be of a piece with his other responses. His is an affirmation of death but without the pathos of the average man or soldier. War is a game for him, exciting and dangerous because a man may strike out or foul out at any time. Such possibilities make both life and war worth the effort expended.

It is tempting and easy to make such a soldier appear more complicated than he is. Much of what I have already made explicit is with him simply implicit and impulse. He does not consciously know why he is careless and lighthearted about his life nor why he sets such value upon new experience. He is what he is for no reason, self-analysis and reflection being among the things he prizes least. Yet his very simplicity is hard to understand. The absence of love as concern for preserving his own and other life makes him seem slightly inhuman. And his innocence of any conventional moral inhibitions, his lack of any real stake in the conservation of existing goods, reinforces this impression.

The soldier as lighthearted adventurer may still be a figure of charm and romance in our modern wars. He possesses what so many lack and wish they had. But he troubles us, too, and especially so when we become reflective. His attitude toward death evokes, I think, our admiration whether we are at peace or war. But his irresponsibility toward society and toward all other values except personal experience cannot but perpetuate most of the evils of our tradition. Frankly, I find myself morally confused by him, both when I knew his like in war and now in memory and meditation. Of one thing I am sure, this kind of soldier or man will be of small service in the struggle to eliminate war. Without wishing it, his nature is too intoxicated by war's promise of intense, forbidden experience.

In some sense, the counterpart of the soldier-adventurer is the more serious professional soldier whose relation to death is governed by the feeling of fate. Death will come to him, he reasons, when the time is ripe and will, he hopes, afford him the opportunity to show himself worthy and unafraid. Sometimes he hopes that death will come to him in full career, that he can die with his boots on, as the phrase has it, for the fatalistic soldier wants to face death as he has faced danger so many times, with a calm, matter-of-fact air. The proper discipline in the event of leaving one's life is, for him, no other than the discipline needed to master life itself. Such a soldier may seem cold and heartless to those around him, without being so in fact. He may be moved deeply enough, but has no intention of letting others see anything that looks like weakness. Duty is, for this professional, the highest value, and courage in performance of his duty is a shining ideal. Death must not be shunned if the interests of duty and honor require it, however unpleasant dying may be. It cannot be avoided, in any event, when your number comes up.

125

Such a soldier cannot be gay or reckless about death, for he has not taken life in that way. But, like the adventurous soldier, he does not consider it alien or apart from his life, either. He seeks to look upon death soberly and objectively, as a normal hazard, to be avoided if possible but never at any cost. Even when such a professional has a premonition of his imminent death, it does not change his actions at all, as the literature of war makes clear. He takes great pride in performing as usual to the end. For example, in a few of the letters from Stalingrad, professional army sons writing to their German fathers, also of high military rank, could not refrain from a formal farewell, taking final leave of their fathers as they would announce, with appropriate salute, their departure for another post. To die was their last mission, and they were on orders here as elsewhere. Never fear that the orders would not be carried out.

It can be said, I think rightly, that this type of soldier has taken death into life and made the end of life a piece with the rest of it. Unlike the carefree adventurer, this is for him customarily a conscious process. He has thought about death and dying, and his discipline in daily life is partly a consequence of this fact. That is, he strives to build up in himself an inner fortress that will be impregnable to the worst assaults. As a professional soldier, he becomes aware early that the trial of death is normally the ultimate trial the military life can ask of its own. Hence he fortifies himself with the sentiments military men have endorsed for ages, again well expressed by Shakespeare, in *Coriolanus*:

> It seems to me most strange that men should fear;
> Seeing that death, a necessary end,
> Will come when it will come.

126

This fatalism about the day and the hour may be thought to be rationalization, a way of making the ordeal easier to bear. But I believe it stems more often than not from other motives. Though others than professional soldiers may be fatalists, of course, this view of death appears to be especially congenial to the military mind. The reason is that the professional soldier feels the need to reduce the capriciousness of his world as much as possible. He chooses to conceive an orderly universe with stable and traditional values, in which death must have its rank and time like everything else. In this attempted reduction of all things to the matter of fact and predictable, the fatalistic soldier does not lose his subjective responses, but they do become subordinated. Hence, when his time comes to die, he tends to be governed by the objective situation more than by his feelings. In effect, he can sometimes say: "My passing is an event, too, like all others to be recorded in the proper 'morning reports.' It would have been predictable had I had the necessary data available." He concludes that there is nothing haphazard about the progress of events, whatever the outward appearance may be.

That the course of war is as wayward and unpredictable as the imaginations of men is a conviction as old as the ancient Pericles. But how many professional military men ever accept it? On the contrary, the world they inhabit, both outer and inner, must be governed by iron laws, and any individual fate is an insignificant part of a universal determinism. It is probably undeniable that dying is easier for one who holds fast to such a faith, but we have no reason to conclude that this is the reason the fatalist holds it.

Much more self-conscious and articulate, yet probably still of the same species, is the relation to death that certain poetic and philosophic natures win through war. For them, the hovering presence of death becomes intimately experienced reality, whereby life gains not only in poignancy but also in creative possibility. Death's finality and certainty can even become a hold and a stay in the threatening chaos of feeling. Perhaps for this reason poets write so much of death, and war poets frequently become obsessed with the subject. They are attracted to death as the moth is to the flame. In the war poems of a Rupert Brooke, for example, death is longed for as the only possibility of giving life authenticity and creative power.

This kind of soldier can gain an intimacy with death denied to the less imaginative. He knows from experience that all creation is a kind of dying, in the sense that every experience to which he has given poetic form has been left behind him forever. In the maelstrom of conflict this soldier believes he is experiencing the very pulse of life in its dedication to death. Sometimes he falls in love with death rather than with life, though when this happens he betrays his creative talents, or at least weakens them, for it is life that is being compressed and intensified and rendered genuine by death's presence. Means and ends dare not be confused here, though they sometimes are. If his creative nature is strong enough to resist the temptations, the poet can frequently find fulfillment of his life in combat, as he might never have found it at home. The heightened awareness of man's transience, vulnerability, and proud courage, which the poet experiences in warfare, can reconcile him to his fate and even promote a love for it.

Philosophical poets, like philosophical soldiers in general, are capable of anticipating death as an adventure in knowledge. This extends also in some cases to the experience of dying. The poet Browning in the well-known poem "Prospice" speaks of dying as "one fight more, the best and the last!" and proclaims himself as a fighter who would not want to have "death bandage his eyes" and bid him creep past. On the contrary, he wants to bear the brunt of the struggle of dying and so anticipate what lies beyond. Such a relationship to death is a combination of heroic acceptance and intellectual eagerness for knowledge. Hence, the philosophical poet can appease both the emotional and intellectual drives of his being. Though the ability to look upon one's own death as a chance to learn what has been hitherto denied may not be widely shared, it is an element, surely, in all the more rational attitudes toward death. There are men with an insatiable curiosity about what it is like to be dead.

The French philosopher Descartes, who spent his youth as a hired soldier under foreign flags, is reported to have said on his deathbed that he was about to experience what he had long eagerly wished to know. And Socrates, who as a soldier had looked death in the face more than once, could not conceal his curiosity about the experience of dying and the possibility of a transformation of life beyond death. The love of knowledge, so rarely found in its pure state, can, nevertheless, impel men of superior mentality to regard death as a boundary they should transgress in order to see whether it in turn may be bounded. For them, the unknown is neither uncanny nor frightening. It is, above all, interesting. Death may hold the solution to the riddles of existence, and something within them will not accept resignation to human finitude. They must burst the bonds and gain some firsthand experience of this encompassing presence into which they see so many entering daily. Such a relation to death can be won in peace as well as in war, I realize, but unless human beings are pushed to the extreme, we are not so likely to confront simple and primal realities.

FIVE

IMAGES

OF THE

ENEMY

I am quite uncertain of the date, and, as a matter of fact, of many other things. But I do know that I am very tired tonight, that it is raining outside, and that I am sitting in a dingy hotel room, somewhere in France, writing this by candlelight—German candlelight, incidentally, since here in France we use much abandoned equipment and food. Sometimes the sheets on the hotel beds don't get changed between German and American occupation. Perhaps last night or night before a German officer sat where I now sit writing to a friend in Germany. Perhaps, too, he is the one I saw lying along the road today with hands neatly folded over the chest, one of the few corpses I have seen who didn't look altogether horrible. And the French officer with me spoke gleefully in German: "So möchte ich sie alle sehen" (I'd like to see them all this way). So is the war here. (War journal, September 12(?), 1944)

The basic aim of a nation at war in establishing an image of the enemy is to distinguish as sharply as possible the act of

131

killing from the act of murder by making the former into one
deserving of all honor and praise. If twentieth-century wars
were not such desperate conflicts, we might be satisfied to
regard destroying the enemy as morally neutral and so avoid
the extreme discontinuity between the morality of war and
peace. In fact, the distinction between taking life in battle at
the command of the state and taking life as a private citizen at
one's own will is a customary distinction with which Western
civilization has managed these many centuries. Unfortunately,
modern war has changed its character so greatly that the old
distinction no longer satisfies. Previously, armed forces and
civilian populations were reasonably distinct. Now, combat
men, particularly artillerymen and fliers, find themselves destroying women and children as well as armed opponents; indeed, whole populations come more and more to be regarded
as legitimate objects of annihilation.

With the disappearance of accepted standards of military
ethics—what we used to call "chivalry"—restraints on the way
the enemy's will to resist is broken down have disappeared.
Even in democratic lands, soldiers are systematically trained
"to fight dirty," which means to disregard all civilian rules
of fair play. "Never give your enemy a chance" is the byword
of this training. The baseness and inhumanity of such tactics
commonly shock the recruit at first, but fear and hatred aid
greatly in their early acceptance. Nowadays, we quickly reach,
by the benefit of propaganda, that terribly simplified morality
with a single absolute: "Any act that helps my side win the
war is right and good, and any act that hinders it is wrong and
bad." This drive toward moral absolutism of a totalitarian sort
affects all other aspects of warfare in our age. Restraints and
restrictions are falling away everywhere. Thus, the typical
image of the enemy is conditioned by the need to hate him

without limits. War has lost its former character of a deadly game, and becomes increasingly a struggle for national survival, in which all moral principles except the one concerning victory are strategic instruments.

Most soldiers are able to kill and be killed more easily in warfare if they possess an image of the enemy sufficiently evil to inspire hatred and repugnance. In this century, when military enemies become friends and friends become enemies with bewildering rapidity, agencies of public opinion are taxed to manipulate mass emotions in ways beneficial to national survival. All forward-looking governments have learned to rate psychological preparations for war as of equal importance, at least, with the physical training of citizens and soldiers. As a consequence, the image of the enemy a contemporary soldier takes with him to the front is certain to be a synthetic product of the mass media, more or less consciously instilled in him by his government to make him a better fighter. When radically altered political needs force a reversal of this image a few years later, governments are greatly aided by modern forgetfulness and bewilderment at the complexity of political change. The capacity of most of us to pursue a continuous thread through the welter of events is severely limited. We strive to keep an equilibrium amid a thousand impressions and to make sense of our world by elimination when it becomes impossible to do so by synthesis. Hence, we can often be persuaded by the mass media to hold an opinion opposite to the one held a few years ago, without remembering that it is the opposite.

We do well to reflect for a moment on the term "the enemy" as it is used in wartime. Its meaning is as protean and diverse as can be, ranging all the way from a purely formal designation of a military adversary to the emotional expression of greatest detestation. Always, the definite article is used with the noun, not *an* enemy or *our* enemy. The implication easily drawn is that the opponent is mankind's enemy as well as ours, and also that this enemy is a specific, though undifferentiated group, an implication that is only pseudo-concrete. That is, by reference to *the* enemy we seem to mean a unified, concrete universal, whereas in fact the enemy is probably not more unified than is our side and possesses many other characteristics than those that are hostile to us. By designating him with the definite article, it is made to appear that he is single and his reality consists in hostility to us. Thus do the moral absolutisms of warfare develop through the medium of language, and, all unconsciously, we surrender reason to the emotional contagion of the communal.

The abstractness of the term promotes in this emotion-drenched atmosphere of war the growth of abstract hatred. I think it is abstract hatred and not the greater savagery of contemporary man that is responsible for much of the blood lust and cruelty of recent wars. This word "abstract" signifies in origin to "draw out from," to take from any larger whole one particular feature or aspect. The opposite of "abstract" is, of course, "concrete," which in its fullest sense still means to examine anything in its entirety, together with its relations to other things. Hence, abstract hatred arises from concentrating on one trait of a person or group while disregarding other features, not to speak of the larger context in which all the traits coexist and modify each other. The simplification of abstract thinking is strictly comparable to the inhumanity of abstract emotions, particularly abstract hatred.

Intellectually, all of us can grant that the reality and truth of a human being can only be found in his total environment, including his past and his inner motives. It is possible to know a person concretely and still hate him, but such hatred is much rarer and of a very different quality. In a sense, hatred is nearly always abstract to some degree, since as a passion it is unable to view anyone or anything in entirety. The hatred that arises for the enemy in wartime, whether it be for Nazis, Communists, or Capitalists, for White, Yellow, or Black, is peculiarly one-sided, for it is a fear-filled image. The enemy is not an individual man or woman, but a hostile power intent upon destroying our people and our lives. Our unreflective response is normally total enmity for the image of evil that possesses our imagination.

As the war progresses, we are hardened and consumed by this hatred of a shadowy image. The farther we are from dangerous contact with this image, the more we are consumed by it. A civilian far removed from the battle area is nearly certain to be more bloodthirsty than the front-line soldier whose hatred has to be responsible, meaning that he has to respond to it, to answer it with action. Many a combat soldier in World War II was appalled to receive letters from his girl friend or wife, safe at home, demanding to know how many of the enemy he had personally accounted for and often requesting the death of several more as a personal favor for her!

Similarly, soldiers who cherished concrete emotions found the moral atmosphere at the front so much more endurable than in rear areas that they willingly accepted the greater strain and personal danger of combat. Progression in abstract hatred was detectable at every level, from company to regiment to division to army and farther back. As one approached the combat area, relations between officers and men became more natural and functional; the spit and polish of army book discipline disappeared. Though I did not understand the reasons then as well as I now do, a letter I wrote in February

1945 expresses the facts of this transformation concisely enough:

> . . . *You would be amazed at the changed aspect of military rules and regulations in frontal areas. Everything assumes a personal aspect. "The book" is pretty much thrown out the window, particularly in the experienced units, and it becomes "Who do you know?" and "What can you get away with?" This is particularly true in our service. There is a surprising lack of orders from above; each man becomes more or less his own authority. The amount of individual responsibility is both frightening and heartening. Some of us have become very resourceful as a consequence, which is, of course, all to the good. . . . The GI aspects have almost all fallen away, and we work with each other from corporals to colonels on pretty much an equal basis. The farther back one is, of course, the less true this becomes.*

Equally important, the enemy, too, seemed nearly human and, like us, tired, and fearful of his life. Reduction of physical distance did not necessarily reduce psychical distance, I suppose, but there was usually a relationship, startling enough in character. To be sure, much of the improvement in spiritual climate was undoubtedly due to the presence of danger and not to a concretizing of the image of the enemy. Hand-to-hand combat grows increasingly rare in our century. Modern weapons keep hostile armies at an ever-greater distance from each other, as a rule. I realize that thousands of soldiers fired incessantly in recent wars without once seeing their targets, and bombardiers destroyed uncounted lives with no conception of the manner of people who were cowering under the falling bombs. Only after a modern war is past and the victorious army is occupying the land of the conquered is the image of the enemy really rendered concrete, and by that time he is likely to be no longer an enemy.

Nevertheless, one opportunity the front-line soldier has to know the enemy as a human being is when he takes prisoners, and this is frequently a crucial experience for soldiers. The prisoner of war reveals to his opponent that he, too, cherishes life and that he has at least a minimal trust in your humanity, otherwise he would not be surrendering. The soldier who has taken, or himself been made, a prisoner of war will inevitably be a changed man and fighter. His foe has been demonstrated to be comprehensible and of the same stuff, at least outwardly, as he himself is made of. I once wrote of this:

While we were waiting there and listening to the sound of the fighting a few hundred yards away, the chatter of machine guns and heavier artillery, German prisoners began to come in. . . . For an hour [I searched them for weapons]. As I talked to these soldiers, I found no hatred for them. . . . But later, when our own infantry soldiers came up the road and advanced into the line, I felt the same attachment to these uncomplaining men who were covered with sweat and grime, had marched far and for many days, fighting most of the way and with few prospects. They were carrying heavy burdens but none complained. Truly, a mad warfare.

An incident that happened in my presence in Italy during the war illustrates perfectly what I have in mind. A certain infantry division, freshly committed to a sector of the front, had transformed its band unit into military police in charge of prisoners of war. I happened to be at the prisoner cage shortly after these music-loving soldiers had received their first batch of prisoners. A group of these youths stood, guns at the ready and very tense, facing the disarmed Germans in a stable of an old farmhouse. They were half expecting the captives at any moment to snarl and spring upon them. As soldiers fresh from the United States, their image of all Germans was that they were treacherous and fanatical storm troopers. For their part, the captured soldiers were apparently glad to be prisoners, though they, too, were apprehensive about the menacing rifles.

We stared at one another with a confused mixture of hostility and fear, all alike victims of ignorance. Suddenly I heard some of the prisoners humming a tune under their breath. Four who were a trained quartet and had contrived to be captured together started to sing. Within a few minutes, the transformation in the atmosphere of that stable was complete, and amusing, too, in retrospect. The rifles were put down, some of them within easy reach of the captives. Everybody clustered closer and began to hum the melodies. Cigarettes were offered to the prisoners, snapshots of loved ones were displayed, and fraternization proceeded at a rapid rate. When the commanding officer, just as new to combat as his men, arrived on the scene, he was speechless with fury and amazement. The contrast between abstract image and this glimpse of reality could hardly have been more striking.

However shadowy and unknown in their essential nature enemy soldiers remain for the man in combat, their physical nearness forces a change in his abstract image of them, even if not necessarily in the way of concreteness. They are no longer one vast and undifferentiated power of evil, but more detached centers of violence and danger who must be resisted and destroyed if possible by himself and comrades. Very often his abstract hatred is changed by degrees into personal hatred. Are they not responsible for the hard, uncomfortable life he is forced to lead? Were it not for them he would be at home with his wife or girl friend, enjoying his favorite food or sport or other amusement. His mood may become one of deep resentment or smoldering anger against the cause of his present misery. He wants to make them pay for this long-continued disruption of his life, "they" being not the enemy in general so much as that group opposite his position at the front. The more cramped, painful, and unbearable his physical and psychological environment becomes, the more he is likely to be filled with a burning vengeance, which demands action for its alleviation.

When the soldier has lost a comrade to this enemy or possibly had his family destroyed by them through bombings or through political atrocities, so frequently the case in World War II, his anger and resentment deepen into hatred. Then the war for him takes on the character of a vendetta. Until he has himself destroyed as many of the enemy as possible, his lust for vengeance can hardly be appeased. I have known soldiers who were avid to exterminate every last one of the enemy, so fierce was their hatred. Such soldiers took great delight in hearing or reading of mass destruction through bombings. Anyone who has known or been a soldier of this kind is aware of how hatred penetrates every fiber of his being. His reason for living is to seek revenge; not an eye for an eye and a tooth for a tooth, but a tenfold retaliation. I described one of these men in my journal:

He said that he would not be happy until every German was killed—said it in a careless, offhand manner and with a laugh told how he was complaining this morning about too many prisoners being brought in and the soldier who had brought one said, "I am doing my best, sir, I started with six!" The others laughed. I thought: It is the fortunes of war. Those who were shot might have expected it. I need not feel sorry for them. But for those who want people killed because it will spare them work and because they cherish revenge . . . for those I feel sorrow and also anger.

. . . Coming up this morning we saw an Italian youth lying in a field close by the road, crumpled up in death. Further on, a German soldier with face black and distended sprawled in death behind a straw stack; farther on still, was a horribly mangled soldier on the road with our vehicles passing over him. There was some artillery fire, and shells landed not far away, but I was not much frightened. Slowly I am becoming insensitive to everything.

Understandable as this hatred is, it would nonetheless be false to think of it as concrete because motivated by personal grievance. Such a soldier's hatred would be concrete only if it were directed toward the immediately guilty party, or group, who was conscious of and responsible for his evil deed. For example, a Jewish soldier might cherish a concrete hatred for the Nazi police charged with persecuting his family and perhaps could concretely hate the convinced members of the whole Nazi party. But the soldier burning with vengeance feelings has commonly made a vast extension of his personal hatred to all who speak the language and wear the uniform of the enemy. To him, they become all alike and to kill one is as good as to kill any other. Hence, he is not fighting men but embodiments of undifferentiated evil. The change in him is not so much a result of a new relationship toward the enemy as it is an emotional response to loss and exposure. He has not really broken through the barrier of the abstract. All that he has done is to give his enmity for the antagonists a new spring from which to drink. Instead of *the* enemy, they have become *my* enemies.

No one should underestimate the cruelty and the delight in cruelty when a soldier—or a civilian—is impelled by such personal, abstract hatred. For this reason, civil wars are usually replete with refinements of personal torture and are commonly more terrible than international wars. Yet, paradoxical as it may seem, personal hatred even of this sort carries with it more possibility of humaneness than does abstract hatred where no personal injury has been suffered and where the hater is without responsibility and not in danger. The combat soldier knows that the figures opposite him are in some sense responsible for his plight, even if they have done him no personal wrong. They would kill him if they could, as they have killed friends of his. Of that he is sure. That they may justly cherish the same sentiments toward him is a possibility that may occur to the combat man at any moment. And this possibility—namely, the justice of the enemy soldier's position vis-à-vis you as an individual—can effect a radical change in the relationship. The recognition of a common humanity, sinful and pathetic, is not at all remote in this situation. Soldiers of opposite sides, dying together in the same shell hole, have frequently transcended their hatred and ended *their* war in reconciliation. Anything is possible through the recognition of your enemy's common humanity, even if it leads to fierce rejection of him. Close friendships have arisen from bitter enmities more than once, and these friendships have been fruitful and especially dear. But from abstract hatred, which remains remote from action and danger, only blank forgetfulness can result and an unrelenting heart which weakens the sympathies of its possessor.

To designate as abstract the usual images of the enemy is, of course, only a beginning toward understanding why men so readily kill and get killed in wartime. Abstractions are of different orders. There were four common attitudes toward the enemy held by soldiers of recent wars. Three of them will be found to be abstract in the extreme, the fourth of a different order altogether. Though separated for purposes of understanding, no one would assert that these attitudes are distinct in individual soldiers. Actually, most of us probably held in the course of our combat service two or more of them, possibly also others that I did not myself experience or observe. Those I want to reflect upon are exceedingly common, and have an important effect not only upon the character of the soldiers cherishing them, but upon the historical situation of our age as well.

One of the most time-honored and persistent images of the enemy, today very suspect in democratic lands, is the one held by the professional soldier, who regards all military men as comrades in arms. What are the essential features of this attitude? It is governed in the first instance by the professional's concept of his task in war. War is his vocation, however hard he may have hoped in long years of peacetime service that it would not come. He is entrusted with a task, or a mission, in military vocabulary, and it is all-important to him that the mission be successfully accomplished. As a technologist of war, the professional asks himself: "How am I to fulfill my mission?" The enemy has to be outwitted, outmaneuvered, and outkilled. He is a human obstacle to be overcome on the way to a clearly defined objective. If the professional is a regular officer of some rank, he has spent the years of peace overcoming an imaginary enemy in simulated campaigns, and this experience dominates his mind on the field of battle. He feels not unlike the captain of a football team pitted against the opponent. The enemy is for him at first only a concentration of capabilities, probable plans, and troop dispositions. To learn as much about him as you can while keeping him ignorant of yourself and your intentions is a fundamental task. For the professional military man, battles are still huge games, man's greatest sport, an ancient feeling he finds diffi-

cult to resist, even if it does conflict with the dominant ideology of our day and even if wars do become less and less
like sports in their consequences.

The professional as a technologist likes to regard himself as
an instrument of the state. Though he has natural sympathies
and antipathies for this or that foreign people, he can suppress
these feelings and adopt a hostile attitude toward any state
not his own—on orders. As an "arm" and not the "head" of
the state, the professional soldier often prides himself on being
nonpolitical. This frees him, he feels, to act in war without
regard for consequences other than the military. Responsibility
must be clearly defined and portioned out; it is always a matter for angry puzzlement on his part that such definition and
apportionment are rarely possible in actual combat. As a
specialist in warfare, he wants none of the half-light and
dubiety of morals and politics in his profession. He desires to
be under orders and to know what is expected of him all the
time. Since war is so much simpler if played according to
rules, he yearns for the security and stability of formal principles in fighting.

His attitude toward his opponent is likely to be at once
simple and complex. In one sense, the enemy is necessary,
and, like Voltaire's God, if he did not exist it would be essential to create him. The true military man is pleased if he has
a resourceful and courageous enemy opposing him. "The next
best thing to a good friend is a good enemy" is no doubt a
saying of military origin. On the other hand, the professional's
scorn for an easily beaten or unskillful foe passes all bounds.
Though he will show a courageous enemy no mercy in combat
so long as that foe possesses destructive power, the military
man is likely to cherish for him respect and even admiration.
Consequently, when he is captured and disarmed, the impulse

143

of the victor is to be magnanimous and friendly. Sensible rules require, according to this code, humane treatment of a surrendering enemy, who a few minutes before was intent on destroying your life and who probably succeeded in blasting life and limbs from numerous soldiers under your command. Such reasoning appears to be crystal clear to a professional mind. The enemy was simply doing his duty, as you are expected to do yours. The more damage he has wreaked, the greater your pride in finally subduing him.

Such a conception antedates, of course, the sentiments of modern nationalism and democracy. It harks back to the days when professional soldiers were mercenaries, serving for the love of fighting as well as for money. Because military organization and thinking appear to be inherently conservative, not to say atavistic, it lingers on to play an important role in our century. In World War II literature we find this image in its pure state in the person of Field Marshal Erwin Rommel. Rommel belonged heart and soul to the professional tradition of the German Army, where this medieval ideal of knighthood (*Ritterlichkeit*) persisted in little-impaired form until the advent of Hitler. Noted for his correct treatment of prisoners, Rommel was frequently outraged by the failure of the Allies to respond in kind. In his professional opponents, he inspired admiration and awe. This is most evident in the well-known book *Rommel, the Desert Fox,* where British author Desmond Young makes an explicit plea for the retention of the tradition that all soldiers of whatever nation are comrades in arms.

The complexity of this image lies in the reversal of attitude toward the enemy as an opponent and as a prisoner. As an armed adversary, he is to be destroyed without mercy. Morally, he has no human status whatever, and no one can hate this enemy so cordially and execrate him so roundly as

144

the professional in pursuit of his aim. The degree of abstraction in his hatred is immense. He is capable of disregarding all other considerations except the single one of destroying everything that stands in the way of successfully accomplishing his mission. He would be the last to grant to himself or his men that the enemy is a human being on the same level as themselves. Yet he is ready to grant it when the enemy is subdued and at his mercy. Generosity and humanity are only possible where there is no equality, where the relation is one of conqueror and conquered. In this the predemocratic nature of the military ideal is apparent.

Often as I have been tempted in reflection to consider this attitude irrational, even absurd, something holds me back. To the professional, it appears self-evident and any other suspect. And since war is actual and real, not merely a concept, this image of the enemy may be preservative of human integrity, as some other images are not. If it regards only one aspect of man, his technical proficiency as a destroyer, it is rational in part and not built of fantasy. The professional does surmise in secret the latent humanity of the opponent as opponent, even if recognition can come only when he is disarmed and helpless or after the war is past.

Actually, many a professional soldier cherishes human sympathy for his opponent even before the decisive battle, but he dare not give it rein lest it incapacitate him for his destructive mission. The understanding of his opponent's motives, a precondition of sympathy, is usually easier for a trained military man than is the comprehension of the motives of his own political superiors or the civilian mentality of his people. Though loyalty is ingrained in him by his professional code, and cannot be easily dislodged, he may discover in himself, if he is reflective, more genuine respect for the enemy he is annihilating than for a great number of those he is risking his life to protect. This commonly recognized fact should surprise nobody, for the military profession, like few others, is a way of life that forms its subjects in relative isolation from modern sentiments and political metamorphoses.

When we ask why this image of the enemy grows increasingly unpopular in our day, honest answers are hardly flattering to the antimilitarists. To be sure, the professional's predilection for regarding war as a game is out of contact with present realities. It violates our moral sense to consider the slaughter and misery of modern wars as anything less than the catastrophe they are. Since they are no longer fought with the weapons of chivalry, and since drafted soldiers are not warriors in the medieval sense, chivalric behavior to the foe appears grotesquely inappropriate. Even if democratic countries find it necessary to use men as means in the wars they fight, it seems degrading to regard them as such, and we therefore resent the military propensity for looking at men as so much material potentiality. In short, the lack of regard for the individual as individual, which is part and parcel of pragmatic military calculation, irritates our modern mentality deeply.

But there is clearly another and more important source for our dislike of this professional image of the enemy. Because our wars are becoming ever more totalitarian in character, this professional attitude is suspect. Increasingly, we cannot fight without an image of the enemy as totally evil, for whom any mercy or sympathy is incongruous, if not traitorous. Our wars are tending to become religious crusades once more, and the crusader's image of the enemy is in sharp opposition to the militarist's.

Curiously enough, General Eisenhower, a professional military man who is very untypical, provides a good example of this attitude toward the enemy. In his *Crusade in Europe* he relates how he refused to follow the urging of some of his staff to allow the captured German General Jürgen von Arnim to call on him, and in this connection explicitly rejects the tradition that all professional soldiers are comrades in arms. "For me," he writes, "World War II was far too personal a thing to entertain such feelings. Daily as it progressed there grew within me the conviction that as never before in a war between many nations the forces that stood for human good and men's rights were this time confronted by a completely evil conspiracy with which no compromise could be tolerated. Because only by the utter destruction of the Axis was a decent world possible, the war became for me a crusade in the traditional sense of that often misused word." It is easy to agree with this evaluation of the Axis powers without drawing the conclusions for personal behavior toward an individual member of those nations that General Eisenhower does. Ironically enough, a few years later he found it necessary to adopt a quite different attitude toward the German soldier of World War II and many German general officers as well.

If the professional soldier reduces the enemy to the status of an object until he is subdued, the crusader denies his humanity by making him into a devil before and for a time after his subjugation. The one might well be regarded as a predemocratic image, the other as a postdemocratic one. It is hard to say which image is more abstract, though certainly the crusader's is destined to be more unrelenting in battle. The military man finds it almost a condition of his vocation that he regard men in terms of force, that is, as objects, and disregard all those subjective factors that distinguish every man from every other. The personality of each man becomes of interest to him, not for itself alone, but for its military effectiveness. Hence, the professional is caught in a world of means and instruments, himself one among others. He makes war a means for furthering political ends, and his preoccupation, like his occupation, is seldom with things for their own sake. This is the abiding curse of the military profession. The total human being has no chance to break through to consciousness because there is no official interest in the whole human being. So the professional image of the enemy is a consequence of the pattern of life imposed on those who serve as instruments and not ends. The abstraction of the image is more or less inevitable.

Equally ancient, and apparently as persistent, is the image of the enemy as a creature who is not human at all. Especially common to simple, uneducated soldiery when fighting a foe of another color or race, it is by no means unknown to educated, unimaginative men. They regard the opponent as subhuman, a peculiar species of animal with indeterminable qualities and habits, all evil. War against him does not, however, become simply a hunt or chase, even though he is hunted down and exterminated wherever possible. The enemy is considered to be a peculiarly noxious kind of animal toward whom one feels instinctive abhorrence. He is often compared to a snake, since most Western peoples feel a superstitious fear and aversion for snakes and attempt to destroy them on sight.

This image of the enemy is fear-filled as no other is, since no one attributes calculable ways of behavior to the foe, but, on the contrary, expects any manner of enormity from him. Though he be animalic in being without human emotions and reason, he is thought to be capable of treachery, recklessness, and blood lust to superhuman extent. Based as it is on ignorance and primitive dread, this image prevents those who hold it from any reasonable calculation of the enemy's actual strength or weakness. If modern soldiers no longer believe in magical powers after the manner of uncivilized peoples, they come perilously close to attributing mysterious potencies to a foe like this.

The obvious, though already painful, example for the United States of this attitude toward the enemy was in our recent war with Japan. Anyone acquainted with the literature of this war realizes how prevalent such an image was in the minds of officers and enlisted men alike. Herman Wouk, in a surprisingly detached comment in *The Caine Mutiny*, tells of the naval battle of Kwajalein and describes the indifference of the Navy men to the suffering of the enemy as follows:

> This cold-bloodedness, worthy of a horseman of Genghis Khan, was quite strange in a pleasant little fellow like Ensign Keith. Militarily, of course, it was an asset beyond price. Like most of the naval executioners at Kwajalein, he seemed to regard the enemy as a species of animal pest. From the grim and desperate taciturnity with which the Japanese died, they seemed on their side to believe they were contending with an invasion of large armed ants. This obliviousness on both sides to the fact that the opponents were human beings may perhaps be cited as the key to the many massacres of the Pacific war.

When soldiers are driven to battle by this image, they are freed from the possibility of remorse for their deeds. Their hunting impulses are released to seek the most dangerous of all beasts and the one most deserving of death. In this sense, war does become a desperate kind of game. The enemy is sought out to be exterminated, not subdued. There is no satisfaction in capturing him and exacting obedience and respect. There is also, of course, no safety in it, since he is held to be incapable of grasping civilized rules of warfare. Therefore the enemy when disarmed and helpless tends to become the object of target practice for the opposing soldiers.

An intelligent veteran of the war in the Pacific told a class of mine a few years ago how his unit had unexpectedly "flushed" a Japanese soldier from his hiding place well behind the combat area. The unit, made up of relatively green troops, was resting and joking, expecting to be sent forward to combat areas. The appearance of this single enemy soldier did not frighten them, because they knew that this particular island had been effectively cleared of Japanese troops. But they seized their rifles and began using him as a live target while he dashed frantically around the clearing in search of safety. The soldiers found his movements uproariously funny and were prevented by their laughter from making an early end of the unfortunate man. Finally, however, they succeeded in killing him, and the incident cheered the whole platoon, giving them something to talk and joke about for days afterward. In relating this story to the class, the veteran emphasized the similarity of the enemy soldier to an animal. None of the American soldiers apparently even considered that he may have had human feelings of fear and the wish to be spared. What puzzled the veteran in retrospect was why his comrades and he found the incident so humorous. Now, a few years later, it appeared to him grisly and cruel enough; at the time, he had had no conscience about it whatever.

This and similar stories by soldiers of World War II in the Pacific make clearer than analysis can the effect of this image on the person holding it. On first reflection, the enemy conceived as beasts might be thought to be morally the most satisfactory of any image, since it avoids feelings of guilt. Granted the fact of war, the pursuit of killing without compunction could be considered the most healthy and rational possible. War will be a dirty job, but with this attitude the compulsion exercised on soldiers to carry out the unpleasant work of extermination will be minimal and bad psychological effects will be reduced both during the operation and in the postwar world. This standpoint has an illusory character, however. The lack of compunction in such taking of life deprives the destroyer of any emotional purgation. Nothing offsets the corrupting influences of fear and hatred with which the business of slaughter is carried out. Consequently, soldiers permeated with this image of their opponent are subject to rapid brutalization. The veteran referred to above was dismayed by his former attitude because he could not now grasp the degree of unrecognized cruelty that had enabled him then not only to participate in the torture of a defenseless human being but also to find the spectacle amusing.

I suspect that at some level of consciousness many of these soldiers recognize their image to be false and that their rationalization is a way of making things easier for themselves. The foreign, strange, and uncanny only partially victimize them. They allow differences in language and customs and perhaps skin color to persuade them that internally the mind, emotions, and soul are also utterly unlike theirs. But nations in the twentieth century are not so isolated and ignorant of each other as previously, and, in addition, there is always a "Tokyo Rose" or similar phenomenon in our wars to contradict the image of the beast.

If soldiers are completely taken in by this image, it is hard to grasp what their reactions must be when as occupation troops they mingle with the pacified and friendly "enemy." Either they keep detached the wartime image and the peacetime reality, which is what often happens apparently, or they experience in moments when memories intrude hidden doubts and regrets at previous cruelty. The enemy could not have changed, they must reason, so quickly from a beast to a likable human being. Thus, the conclusion is nearly forced upon them that they have been previously blinded by fear and hatred and the propaganda of their own government. Rarely does the veteran need to take the blame on himself to any great extent, since the psychical cost is too great. But his bewilderment at the experience of warfare is surely all the greater.

As important as these moral effects and closely related to them are what might be called the anesthetic effects of this image of the enemy. The ugliness of war against an enemy conceived to be subhuman can hardly be exaggerated. There is an unredeemed quality to battle experience under these conditions which blunts all senses and perceptions. Traditional appeals of war are corroded by the demands of a war of extermination, where conventional rules no longer apply. For all its inhumanity, war is a profoundly human institution, and to be satisfying in any sense, it must retain peculiarly human aspects. Yet this image of the enemy as beast lessens even the satisfaction in destruction, for there is not proper regard for the worth of the objects destroyed. In the recent war against Japan, not only was the fear of death increased because few prisoners were taken and torture of the helpless was common, but also the compensations, the joys of comradeship, keenness of perception, and sensual delights were lessened.

Though Pacific veterans can speak with greater authority than I, it is probable that the war against Japan was particularly revolting not because the terrain on which it was fought was treacherous and unsuited for conventional warfare. It was ugly because the image of the enemy, apparently on both sides, was so far removed from reality. No aesthetic reconciliation with one's fate as a warrior was likely because no moral purgation was possible. Thousands of veterans can testify to days that were grim and relentless and terrible, utterly without beauty and almost without human quality of any sort. At moments the novel *The Naked and the Dead* catches this hideous ugliness of World War II in the East in unforgettable fashion.

There is another image of the enemy closely related to this one, yet even more abstract and deadly in its psychological effects. In this the enemy is conceived to be not merely a loathsome animal, below the human level, but also above it in being a devil or at least demon-possessed and, as such, an enemy of God. Here his humanity is not questioned, for a devil ranges the scale of possibilities from the subhuman to the superhuman. Yet the enemy as devil never achieves the human level because of his will to evil or because he is possessed. The modern soldier who is totalitarian in his thinking, a devoted follower of communism or fascism, feels perhaps more intensely than did the Moslem of medieval times that he is on the side of the divine. His mission is extermination of those who oppose the truth, and it is a holy mission. The enemy in trying to destroy the only revealed truth, the only moral order, the chosen nation, embodies the very essence of evil, which is the devil, or at best he is possessed of some demonic power which renders him incapable of perceiving what is plain as day to the faithful. The enemy, in short, is in revolt against God, interpreted as modern political religions understand God, namely, their highest value.

To be sure, there is considerable difference in the effect of this image upon the soldier if "the Fascist beasts" or "the Communist dogs" or "the Capitalist hyenas" are regarded as inherently incapable of conversion because their nature is to be devilish or if they are regarded as merely possessed. In the former case, there is nothing to do but annihilate them. Killing them becomes a kind of sacrament; after enough of it, the killers come to feel like high priests. Where the enemy is thought to be possessed only, it is permitted to make him prisoner, so that he can be confronted with the truth, before which even devils sometimes yield. Though this latter interpretation moderates one's hatred of the enemy to some extent, it does not change greatly its fanatical, abstract character. In combat the foe possessed of the devil is as wholly treacherous as the foe who is a devil. Both are unworthy to continue in existence when they make war against soldiers who are fighting for truth and right.

Let us look at this totalitarian image of the antagonist in war more closely, for it is fateful in the wars of our day and, alas, does not belong only to states and governments that are dictatorships. The image is abstract to a degree hardly equaled in other images because it refuses to see any quality of the foe except his ideology. It has no interest whatsoever in the concrete differences that may be found in his ranks, nor does it care to seek out causes for demon possession or to understand why creatures who are capable of being men have chosen to be devils. Indeed, the most characteristic aspect of this image is its utter disregard for the individuality of the foe. If this refusal to individualize the enemy is characteristic of all hostile attitudes, only in this totalitarian one is it made into a principle. The fanaticism of the totalitarian soldier lies in his terrible pure-mindedness, in which none of the complicated mixtures of motives that characterize ordinary human life and action are allowed to intrude. His image of the enemy is a logical consequence of his own dogmatic certainty about being in the right. He is insulated against other truth in a way that stupidity or ignorance could never insulate because his reason has been made captive and all experience is made to conform to the revelation that pervades his emotional and intellectual life. Experience is confirmatory and no longer exploratory. Only that part of it is digested which accords with the soldier's grasp of reality.

When the enemy devils do not behave in the fashion conceived to be their true nature, the totalitarian soldier is not tempted to revise his dogmas. On the contrary, he is simply driven to discover motives for their behavior other than the apparent ones. Like all devils, the enemy is deceiving and deceitful. He can feign mercy or fairness in order to catch the foolish and innocent off guard. Since his actions are never to be taken at face value, trust cannot be accorded him. Only eternal suspicion and vigilance are pathways to safety.

All this is heightened when the totalitarian fighter, as commonly happens, conceives that the enemy is not responsible for his devilish nature. For the rational mind, the absence of freedom in the forming of the individual predisposes to mildness and tolerance in his punishment. But something like the reverse is true for the totalitarian fanatic. If the enemy soldiers are driven forward by a power outside themselves to war against God's truth, there is no need to feel sorry for them or to spare them. Since they are determined by this evil principle and are not free agents, they cannot be happy or content in their present state. In theological terms, devils are all creatures of God and cannot complain when He sends his angels to eradicate them in His own good time. Is He not permitted to do what He likes with His own?

The abstractness involved in this image is a double one, as I have tried to point out. The enemy is not regarded as an individual, but a representative of a principle of evil, and he

155

is only an embodiment of this principle. His image is generalized and terribly simplified, resulting in enmity in battle that is probably unsurpassed. One cannot hate subhuman creatures, however vile, so cordially as one hates the violator of a religious image. An extreme in human separation is here reached which shakes the foundation of the personality. When two totalitarian powers make war on each other, the anger and hatred that arise can be appeased only by the death of one or the other. More than this, such killing is profoundly satisfying. Anger and hatred are "fulfilled" in destruction insofar as such emotions know satiety. The more lives the soldier succeeds in accounting for, the prouder he is likely to feel. To his people he is a genuine hero and to himself as well. For him, war is in no sense a game or a dirty mess. It is a mission, a holy cause, his chance to prove himself and gain a supreme purpose in living. His hatred of the enemy makes this soldier feel supremely real, and in combat his hatred finds its only appropriate appeasement.

A skeptic may doubt whether many men are really capable of clinging to such an image of the enemy. Are we not here dealing with an insignificant number of soldiers in any war? I do not think so. Western history has seen many armies in which this image of the foe was widespread, from the days of the Old Testament, where, indeed, the opponent was nearly always regarded as an enemy of Jehovah, to the contemporary Communists. Many believe that the Age of Enlightenment put an end to religious wars in the West, but they have reappeared in political form with a vengeance in the twentieth century. When voluntary German SS troopers engaged fanatic Communists in Russia in World War II, a climax in enmity and hatred was reached in which all traces of chivalry vanished and all moderation was utterly abandoned. Even to read about

some of those battles with an attempt at imaginative understanding is sufficient to shake anyone to the depths. In peacetime surroundings, such murderous hatred is hardly convincing, and fact melts into fable in our endeavor to make the
past believable in the present. Yet even in these battles, the
ultimate was not reached because the majority of soldiers on
both sides were unconvinced of their official faiths; emotionally, they were far from fanatic Nazis and Communists.

It is probably true that most men are incapable of support-
ing over a long period the devil image of the enemy. It
requires an imperviousness to common sense and daily experience, which many are fortunately unable to gain. The dark
vision of Armageddon, which has been an ultimate possibility
for many centuries and which is essentially a religious war
with the devil image of the foe, may hopefully remain a
vision merely. With present technological advances, such a
war could only result in the virtual extinction of life on our
planet and possibly the destruction of the planet itself.

There is, however, no cause for satisfaction in the fact, if,
indeed, it is a fact, that most men are incapable of holding
the devil theory of the enemy for an extended time. The United
States and Russia have come dangerously close in recent years
to that extreme of estrangement where each regards the other
as the enemy of the divine. In the United States, a generation
is growing up without personal contact with anyone of Communist faith. How abstract their image of the Communist is,
only those of us can guess who broach the subject in our
classrooms. It would come as a profound surprise to these
young Americans if they could *see* an educated Communist
discussing his faith in a conventional classroom or lecture hall.
What he said would be less important than a view of him. In
Russia, the image of the American capitalist exploiter is even

more distorted and unreal. If a world war were really to come at this stage, it would be fatally easy to propagate religious fury among masses of men who are already half persuaded. At the moment this is written there is hope that the two systems will come to tolerate more concrete knowledge of each other and thus abate the intolerable danger of a religious war.

The worst effect of absorbing this image is probably not the contraction of personality and outlook which its unreality entails, bad as that is. Those who hold this image of the enemy attest the fact that it is not wholly abstract and unreal. Men *are* capable of being possessed by an evil spirit, or a devil, if one likes to use a metaphor, and, though it is not their whole nature, an impartial judgment must concede that this possession requires fierce resistance if it is to be overcome. The worst effect is that it usually instills in the soldier a conception of himself as avenging angel. The self-satisfaction of such a soldier, his impenetrable conceit, makes him essentially incapable of growth. He is caught in a vise of sterile self-admiration. His ego expands in direct proportion as his bigotry increases. Insulated against experience and free reflection, he is more or less an automaton without ever suspecting it. Neither his hatred of the enemy nor his satisfaction with himself is organic and natural; on the contrary, both are mechanical and pathological. Only a profound shock can convert him from the idea of himself that his image of the enemy has done so much to implant.

The image of the enemy which appeals most to reasonable men after a war is past can be cultivated while war is in progress only by the minority of combat soldiers who are at the same time reflective and relatively independent in their judgment. I refer to the image of the opposing enemy as an essentially decent man who is either temporarily misguided by false doctrines or forced to make war against his better will and desire. The foe is a human being like yourself, the victim of forces above him over which he has no control. Since this image is a concrete one, the soldier who possesses this image does not think in terms of *the* enemy, but recognizes similar differences of opinion and temperament in the opposing forces as in his own. In fact, he is most likely to have gained it through observation of his own comrades. He reasons that people are much alike all over the world, and only an accident of history has made the soldier across the front into a foe rather than an ally. More important than this is his intuitive certainty that closer acquaintance with enemy soldiers would reveal that they have reasons of their own for fighting which must seem to them compelling. The more he is aware of historical causes and the guilt of both sides for hostilities, the greater is his capacity to feel justification for his foe.

Even when such a soldier is deeply convinced that his enemies are motivated by false notions of the mission of their land or ideology and must be defeated at all costs, he feels that these notions are explainable in terms of their history or by the duplicity and evil genius of their leadership. After the shock of defeat, they will require re-education to come once more into peaceful ways. He reasons that many of those across the front are quite clear about the injustice of their cause. But they are caught in a painful dilemma, and must either fight or be disgraced and possibly executed. Or they fight for love of their fatherland, from ignorance of the true causes of the war, or simply because they do not know what else to do, like so many in the soldier's own army. The vast majority of them are thought to be victims of evil leadership.

This is the image of the enemy that many governments encourage at the beginning of wars in our day. Government agencies proclaim that they have no quarrel with the populace as such, only with their political leaders. To be sure, this is sometimes a propaganda device to bring disunion to enemy countries, but it has also been an image held in good faith by large numbers of people. After all, it is easier for a people who have had a reasonably happy history to believe that they are not hated by the rank and file of another nation than it is to believe the opposite. Many soldiers enter the battle zone with the secret belief that their opponent does not really desire to end their lives. Perhaps these soldiers have been in the enemy country under happy auspices and know for themselves that the foe is human and likable. Possibly they have learned to cherish some of his customs, music, and literature. A German making war upon a Frenchman or an American upon an Italian, to cite only two examples, finds it difficult at first to hold any other image than this, for he is likely to have relatives or at least acquaintances in the camp of the enemy.

However, there is a deep contradiction in this attitude which makes its retention for the combat soldier extremely difficult. How is the misguided enemy to be reformed by the use of bullets? If he is a victim of *force majeure*, how can he be liberated from his leaders without destroying him? It is nearly impossible for a combat soldier to prepare himself psychologically for bloody combat with a will to victory while holding such an image of his foe. How can he become enthusiastic about Operation Killer or look forward with eagerness to carrying out a superior's command to close with the enemy? The war itself is more likely to seem the greatest folly and criminality ever perpetrated. If he kills, he is troubled by conscience, and if he does not do his share in the communal life imposed by combat, he is also tormented. The soldier who is on the borders of his own country, fighting against an invading enemy, can more easily find the will to oppose the intruders, but in modern wars it more often happens that he is asked to enter combat on faraway shores and in unfamiliar lands.

Professional officers readily perceive the military disadvantages of this view of the foe and oppose it, as a rule, with passion. If victory is to be achieved, the enemy must be hated by the soldiery to the utmost limit. Hence his character is painted as black as possible and his reputed mercilessness exaggerated on all sides. Professional officers consider part of the psychological training of their troops to be training in hatred, and this becomes more systematized and subtler as the war goes on. The identification between leaders and followers in the enemy ranks soon becomes a dominant theme of the propaganda on both sides. In World War II, for example, all Germans became Nazis, all Japanese fanatic Shintoists, for the Germans all Russians became Communists and all Americans, for their enemies, were bloated imperialists or dupes of satanic Jews. War has its own logic, as I have already emphasized, and such a transformation doubtless requires little conscious directing. The humane image of the enemy is increasingly combated in our century by field commanders of both democratic and totalitarian lands. Perhaps the professionals themselves are more torn than we know by the double image of the enemy as devil on the one hand and a comrade in arms on the other. But their long training enables them to suppress on order all sympathy for their opponents and destroy them without mercy at the proper time.

There is an instructive passage in Tolstoi's *War and Peace* where Kutusov, the Russian general who defeated Napoleon, speaks to a segment of his troops who are relentlessly pursuing

161

and destroying the broken Grande Armée. Mounted on his horse, the old general, whom Tolstoi depicts as a combination of professional soldier and kindly grandfather, is made to speak as follows:

"You see, brothers, I know it's hard for you, but it can't be helped. Bear up; it won't be for long now! we'll see our visitors off and then we'll rest. The Tsar won't forget your services. It is hard for you but still you are at home while they—you see what they have come to," said he, pointing to the prisoners. "Worse off than our poorest beggars. While they were strong, we did not spare ourselves, but now we may even pity them. They are human beings, too. Isn't it so, lads?"

Then he looks perplexed for a few moments, in Tolstoi's account, suddenly changes his whole demeanor, and finishes his speech:

"But after all who asked them here? Serves them right, the bloody bastards!" he cried suddenly, lifting his head. And flourishing his whip he rode off at a gallop for the first time during the whole campaign.

The rational soldier will perceive the illogic of this attitude and reject it for himself. The enemy cannot be at the same time human beings in need of sympathy and "bloody bastards." To the man who sees the enemy as misguided individuals, the Kutusovs are the victims of a military code that is deeply inimical to him. Yet he is certain to be even more alienated from the other views of the enemy, as animals and as devils. He can understand the soldier who possesses a deep personal hatred and a longing for revenge because of wrongs suffered, even if he shudders sometimes at the inhumanity of his rages. But the other views are incomprehensible to him, based as they are on magic and primitive superstition. He would like to believe that these images could be expelled through more knowledge and genuine education, but he is unsure because the power of blind passion has been demonstrated daily in his war experiences.

The combat soldier who refuses to yield to abstract hatred in forming an image of the enemy is accordingly isolated and lonely on a modern battlefield. Often he will wonder why he did not yield to earlier impulses and declare himself a pacifist and conscientious objector to the senseless cruelties of warfare. Since an absolutist position is overwhelmingly popular in wartime, he is quite certain that, if a choice must be made, he belongs to the absolute pacifists as opposed to the apostles of total destruction. Yet he feels himself opposed to both extremes. Normally, he believes enough in the rightness of his country's cause and the wrongness of the opponent to fight and give his life if need be for that conviction. That many innocent victims must suffer and die as a consequence of the struggle for a limited justice is for him an ancient lesson of history with which he can cope in some fashion. It is not the suffering and dying that sickens him so much as it is the brutalization of the emotions and the corruption of the heart which prolonged fighting brings. I could not escape it:

I know that I hate my work in this war, that the war itself is slowly attempting to destroy all that I hold jealously as my own. When I read tonight in the Voelkischer Beobachter, *which was captured on a prisoner, the words of a German soldier's diary, that he had lost his "Ich," his personality in the long years of this war, I shuddered. He spoke for me. . . . Formerly I tried to be mild and kind, now I interrogate the miserable civilians and take pride in sternness and indifferency to their pleas. Perhaps the worst that can be said is that I am becoming a soldier.*

We broke the glass on the door and unbolted the door from the inside. . . . [The Nazi who had committed suicide was]

163

sprawled in a corner dead, a bullet through his temple. It was a pitiless spectacle, but not particularly moving for me. I took his revolver and left him. . . . I felt that his end was just and the solution of a problem. Somehow I have grown quite hard in the past months. . . . God in Heaven, help me to keep my humanity. . . .

The pacifist who refuses to bear arms may not deny the moral superiority of one cause over the other, but he will not grant that violence can determine or establish that superiority. War as a means is to him worse than the evil it seeks to eliminate. If the rational soldier trusted his emotions more, he would concur wholeheartedly with this doctrine. Surely, war is the worst possible way to resolve man's problems. Better than any pacifist, he knows after a few months in combat the essential evils of war. But the voice of reason will contradict his sympathies, assuring him that the pacifist renunciation of the outer self and retreat to some stronghold of inner freedom and resistance is no answer to this world's woes. He can be assured, his reason whispers, that his place is in the midst of it all. If he is forced to do more evil than the pacifist could endure, he is also in a position to accomplish more good. His guilt is heavy, but there is a chance to atone for it here; at home or in some camp for conscientious objectors, there would be none.

Such a soldier knows no peace or security of mind in war. The middle ground that he has chosen is unstable, for the extremes threaten to overwhelm him. It is not only a conflict between reason and emotion, for reason has a powerful voice in some situations in war on the side of pacifism. Increasingly as the war progresses, his choices seem choices among evils, and the greater and lesser evils harder and harder to discern. He longs for the end of the war, when reconciliation with the foe can begin and when he can help to reconstruct what he has had a hand in destroying. Sometimes he longs for death as the only way out of the inextricable web of events, the responsibility for which he partly shares. If the moral enormities of war preoccupy him too exclusively, it is partly because the majority of his fellows seem oblivious to moral considerations. His insistence upon a concrete image of the enemy is responsible for the conflicts of conscience in which he is entangled. Were he able to choose the easier way of his comrades, the battlefield would lose half its horror. As I wrote:

How tired of this war I have got so quickly. It breaks my heart to see these Italian homes broken up, miserable people, shivering and naked, torn from all they have in this world. Where is the end?

How I feel about Allied occupation of Italy is difficult to say. When I see, as yesterday, an American soldier walking down the street holding the hands of two Italian children who in turn held two others by the hand, I feel that all will yet be well. But when I hear how 5th Army CIC in Mondragone is dominated by a cigar-smoking agent who constantly yells: "Hit the f—— bum in the mouth," and "Throw the guinea in the clink," and similar expressions, I grow doubtful.

The concrete image of the enemy is compatible with the limited war of an earlier day. A soldier holding it then might have fought with relative cheerfulness and perhaps regarded war as a confused but not contradictory pattern of human life. Since his view of human nature is realistic, he would possess the virtue of patience with the slow processes of history. What overwhelms his modern counterpart is the antihuman character of total war in our generation. The reasonable soldier is unable to grasp the total unreasonableness of abstract hatred and fanaticism. Absolute virtue and absolute vice are as unreal to him as collective innocence or guilt. He has his limits, this conscientious soldier, both of sympathy and understanding,

165

and modern war exceeds these limits. Consequently, he is a lost soul in total warfare and in global war. There is no place for him at home or in prison, in pacifist work camp or in the military machine. Unless nations return to old-fashioned ways of war and peace, he will be able to breathe freely and move in his proper atmosphere only when modern nations renounce war altogether.

How many soldiers hold these images of the enemy in a modern war? This question is unanswerable, of course. The image in many cases will be, or become, a composite one, with little of the sharp distinctness I have found necessary to make in analysis. Yet this last image is compounded much more rarely with the other three than they are with each other. This image is a reflective one, and he who has learned to think concretely will not hate abstractly, at least not for long. This image alone holds large hope for the future. The question pregnant with possibility is: Can we not expect under modern conditions of communication and transmission of knowledge that realistic attitudes toward potential enemy nations will increase and fewer individuals will be able to generate beast and devil images? This is inseparably connected with the future of war.

I have heard it said in Germany of late that another war between France and Germany is unthinkable because the two peoples have come to know each other so intimately that hostility sufficient for war could no longer be propagated. The assertion is often broadened to include all the countries of Western Europe. By virtue of travel and manifold communications of every sort since the last war, they have come so close to each other that another conflict of European states could not happen. The reasoning behind these statements is that former abstract images and hatreds have gradually given way to concrete knowledge and even friendship. Nowadays adjacent peoples know each other better than did inhabitants of neighboring cities in the same nation a generation ago. The argument appears to be a reasonable one. No one would deny that the world's peoples are coming closer to each other in the sense of physical contacts and at least superficial knowledge of each others' customs, origins, and aspirations. Will it not be increasingly difficult for governments to create a believable image of the beast or the devil in respect to other peoples?

Let us hope so. But I am not too confident. Physical nearness provides us no assurance of understanding or genuine closeness of spirit. Often enough, classes within a country have lived together for hundreds of years and remained exceedingly ignorant of each other. Examples abound in the world today. If civil wars are not as numerous as formerly, is it not more because governments have learned to make better use of secret police, who detect trouble signs early, than because hostility has lessened? We are likely to judge relations among groups too externally and to put great confidence in the appearance of things. I met many who hated their own people with a fierce hatred:

Last evening four of us went to the house of a French lady who spoke English. She and her mother live in a pleasant villa in St. Raphael. . . . To hear her speak of the work of the French underground and how they were killing French collaborators made one's flesh creep. There is no question that the French hate with the greatest bitterness. She spoke with delight of a coming event, supposed to take place today, when forty French girls who had been too friendly with the Germans were to have their heads shaved in public by the Maquis and other Resistance groups. She seemed, and was, a charming lady, but how brutally she spoke of France's enemies!

167

These people live on hatred. What they can do to their victims is almost unbelievable. They carry around with them horror pictures of German atrocities committed on Resistance groups. They feed themselves on hatred. It is all strange and horrible. Death is in the very air here and things far worse than death. . . . I think, too, that there is no religion here, no piety. It is perhaps a great error to think, as we all have, that suffering brings humility and piety.

Yet we know upon reflection that only the slow, unpredictable development of conscientiousness and concern for others brings us close to them, not mere acquaintance and surface intercourse, not mere knowledge. When we ask whether our generation knows more friendship and concern for other peoples than did our forefathers, our answers become hesitant. The pathway to a more peaceful world lies hidden in very complex motives of the human heart. The capacity for compassion and for tolerance of the immense differences among individuals and peoples is only one of the conditions that are important. Another is the strength and insight to recognize our individual freedom and consequent responsibility for our deeds in war and peace.

Few things are more revealing about man as warrior than his tendency to slough off responsibility for the suffering and tragedy he inflicts. And if we could read aright the portent of this absence of guilt feelings in most modern soldiers, it would not be difficult to predict what is yet in store for us in the twentieth century. Why can men do together without conscience things that would torment them unendurably if done singly?

Seated in our living rooms, remote from action and passion, most of us like to believe that we shall never yield again to abstract hatreds. We take pride in feeling our independence of the mass media, and easily persuade ourselves that we are our own men. Many of us are, indeed, impervious to the worst aspects of mass hysteria; we cannot readily be won by the insistent voices of radio, newspaper, and television screen, though hitherto we have always been swept along with the others. Historically, our record for stemming the tide has not been good, and to me, at least, this is a sobering thought. Do we not have a penchant for overestimating our strength in times of crisis, we moderates?

Perhaps even worse, few of us ever know how far fear and violence can transform us into creatures at bay, ready with tooth and claw. If the war taught me anything at all, it convinced me that people are not what they seem or even think themselves to be. Nothing is more tempting than to yield oneself, when fear comes, to the dominance of necessity and to act irresponsibly at the behest of another. Freedom and responsibility we speak of easily, nearly always without recognition of the iron courage required to make them effective in our lives.

SIX

THE ACHE

OF GUILT

*The man I interrogated and took to Army proved to be a spy. . . .
I went to Army two days later, after he had been "broken" by
endless interrogation and considerable beating. . . . It recalled the
memory of Scarpelini in Italy, whom I also apprehended and
turned over. . . . One thing contents me, that these were not innocent soldiers. They knew what they were facing. The German
had been an idealistic Nazi for fifteen years. . . . Am I responsible
for their deaths? Both might well have escaped had it not been
for me. . . . Certainly they had blood on their hands, and desired
to have more. Is their blood on mine? But I am more fortunate
than many soldiers who must kill more innocent men. Perhaps
the hardest thing of all is that I feel no guilt. (War journal,
November 4, 1944)*

Nothing revolts the sensitive spirit so much as the bloody
and unjust deeds of warfare that leave no trace of guilt in the

171

doers and are from every human perspective unavenged. If we were not accustomed to evasions of responsibility in ourselves, such behavior would force us into cynicism of the most nihilistic sort or, at the best, to complete bewilderment about human nature. Yet a voice within each of us echoes the sentiments of Hamlet: "Use every man after his desert, and who should 'scape whipping?"

The fighting man is disinclined to repent his deeds of violence. Men who in private life are scrupulous about conventional justice and right are able to destroy the lives and happiness of others in war without compunction. At least to other eyes they seem to have no regrets. It is understandable, of course, why soldiers in combat would not suffer pangs of conscience when they battle for their lives against others who are trying to kill them. And if the enemy is regarded as a beast or a devil, guilt feelings are not likely to arise if he is slain by your hand. But modern wars are notorious for the destruction of nonparticipants and the razing of properties in lands that are accidentally in the path of combat armies and air forces. In World War II the number of civilians who lost their lives exceeded the number of soldiers killed in combat. At all events, the possibilities of the individual involving himself in guilt are immeasurably wider than specific deeds that he might commit against the armed foe. In the thousand chances of warfare, nearly every combat soldier has failed to support his comrades at a critical moment; through sins of omission or commission, he has been responsible for the death of those he did not intend to kill. Through folly or fear, nearly every officer has exposed his own men to needless destruction at one time or another. Add to this the unnumbered acts of injustice so omnipresent in war, which may not result in death but inevitably bring pain and grief, and the impartial observer may wonder how the participants in such deeds could ever smile again and be free of care.

The sober fact appears to be that the great majority of veterans, not to speak of those who helped to put the weapons and ammunitions in their hands, are able to free themselves of responsibility with ease after the event, and frequently while they are performing it. Many a pilot or artilleryman who has destroyed untold numbers of terrified noncombatants has never felt any need for repentance or regret. Many a general who has won his laurels at a terrible cost in human life and suffering among friend and foe can endure the review of his career with great inner satisfaction. So are we made, we human creatures! Frequently, we are shocked to discover how little our former enemies regret their deeds and repent their errors. Americans in Germany after World War II, for instance, feel aggrieved that the German populace does not feel more responsibility for having visited Hitler upon the world. The Germans, for their part, resent the fact that few Americans appear to regret the bombing of German cities into rubble and the burning and crushing of helpless women and children. It appears to be symptomatic of a certain modern mentality to marvel at the absence of guilt consciousness in others while accepting its own innocence as a matter of course.

No doubt there are compelling historical reasons why soldiers in earlier times have felt comparatively little regret for their deeds and why modern soldiers in particular are able to evade responsibility so easily. It is wise to assume, I believe, that the soldiers who fight twentieth-century wars are morally little better or worse than their grandfathers or great-grand-fathers in previous wars. Nevertheless, there are some novel factors in our time that, taken together with the traditional ways of escape, make it easier for the majority of soldiers to

173

carry the guilt for the destruction of the innocent in contemporary conflicts. These novel factors lie both in our contemporary interpretation of guilt and in the nature of recent combat.

Our age seems peculiarly confused about the meaning of guilt, as well as its value. With the rise of modern psychology and the predominance of naturalistic philosophers, guilt has come to be understood exclusively in a moral sense. Its older religious and metaphysical dimensions have been increasingly forgotten. Moreover, these naturalistic psychologists have tended to view guilt feelings as a hindrance to the free development of personality and the achievement of a life-affirming outlook. They like to trace guilt to the darker, subconscious levels of the soul and emphasize its backward-looking character as opposed to the future-directed impulses of the natural man. Hence guilt, when reduced to moral terms, has more and more been branded as immoral. To some, it is associated with a species of illness, which must be cured by psychiatric treatment. Though these modern doctors of the soul realize that the uninhibited man is not an attainable ideal, they still strive for the goal of acceptance of oneself and one's nature for what they are. The individual is released as far as possible from regret for past deeds and from the hard duty to improve his character.

Even if these doctrines get modified in actual practice and are seldom read in their deeper meanings, the basic ideas filter into the broadest strata of our population and help to form the dominant mood of our day. Even the simplest soldier suspects that it is unpopular today to be burdened with guilt. Everyone from his pastor to his doctor is likely, if he brings up feelings that oppress him, to urge him to "forget it." Precisely this is what he often longs to hear, and, so, forgetting becomes such a disquieting phenomenon of the modern mind.

In war itself, the most potent quieters of conscience are evidently the presence of others who are doing the same things and the consciousness of acting under the orders of people "higher up" who will answer for one's deeds. So long as the soldier thinks of himself as one among many and identifies himself with his unit, army, and nation, his conscience is unlikely to waken and feel the need to respond. All awareness of guilt presupposes the capacity to respond as an individual to the call of conscience. I am using the term "respond" in its original meaning of answer to a question or a demand made on the self. We respond to conscience only when we can separate ourselves from others and become conscious, often painfully so, of our differentness. Though the call of conscience may seem to be an impersonal voice outside of one, the response is peculiarly within the individual self. Why did *you* do this? Why did *you* not do that? If we hear at all and if we attempt to answer, the response must begin with the first person singular pronoun. I must begin with myself as I was:

My conscience seems to become little by little sooted. . . . If I can soon get out of this war and back on the soil where the clean earth will wash away these stains! I have also other things on my conscience. . . . [A man named H., accused of being the local Gestapo agent in one small town] was an old man of seventy. His wife and he looked frightened and old and miserable. . . . I was quite harsh to him and remember threatening him with an investigation when I put him under house arrest. . . . Day before yesterday word came that he and his wife had committed suicide by taking poison. Fain and I went back and found them dead in their beds, he lying on his back and reminding me, gruesomely enough, of my father, she twisted over on her side with her face concealed. At the bedside was a card on which he had scrawled: "Wir mussten elend zu Grunde gehen. Der Herr Gott verzeihe uns. Wir haben niemandem leid getan.". . . [We must perish miserably.

God forgive us. We have done no one any harm.] The incident affected me strongly and still does. I was directly or indirectly the cause of their death. . . . I hope it will not rest too hard on my conscience, and yet if it does not I shall be disturbed also.

Since conscience normally awakens in guilt in the sense that a troubled conscience is usually our first indication of its existence, it is clear that an important function of guiltiness is to make us aware of our selves. Whatever his response, the person who hears the call of conscience is aware of freedom in the form of a choice. He could have performed differently than he did; an act of his might have been different. The whole realm of the potential in human action is opened to him and with it the fateful recognition that he is in charge of his own course. Conscience is thus in the first instance a form of self-consciousness. It is that form that gives to us an unmistakable sense of free individuality and separates for us the domains of the actual and the ideal. Therewith the life of reflection begins, and the inner history of the individual no longer corresponds to his outer fate.

But the individual need not waken, and, indeed, everything in warfare conspires against such response to the call of freedom. Enemy and ally enclose his little life, and there is little privacy or escape from their presence. Loyalty to his unit is instilled by conscious and unconscious means; the enemy is seeking to destroy that unity and must be prevented from doing so at all costs. He is one with the others in a fraternity of exposure and danger. His consciousness of the others may be vague but is an omnipresent reality; it has much similarity to dream awareness. Directly, he is aware of his pals, the half-dozen or more men he knows relatively well, with a few dozen more who are on the periphery of his consciousness. Beyond them there are thousands who encircle him, whose presence he senses. There is a vast assemblage of unknown "friends" confronting an equally vast mass of unknown "enemies," and he is in the midst of all of them. Their presence makes his situation endurable, for they help to conquer the loneliness that oppresses him in the face of death, actual or possible. Something within him responds powerfully to the appeal of the communal. The orders that he receives from those in charge of his fate hold him where he is in the midst of disorder. He is compelled and controlled as though by invisible threads through the unseen presence of the others, friend and foe.

In an exposed position on the battlefield during action, his consciousness of being a part of an organism is likely to plunge him into contradictory feelings of power and impotence which succeed one another rapidly. "If I don't hit that guy out there or man this machine gun to the last, my buddies will be killed and I'll be the cause of their death. Everything depends on me." A few minutes later he is likely to ask himself what one rifle or machine gun on one tiny portion of the field can possibly matter to the final outcome. His place in the whole complex is lost to sight, and he is in danger of feeling how absolute is his dependence. All the time, he acts as he feels he must, swept by moods of exultation, despair, loyalty, hate, and many others. Much of the time he is out of himself, acting simply as a representative of the others, as part of a superpersonal entity, on orders from elsewhere. He kills or fails to kill, fights courageously or runs away in the service of this unit and unity. Afterward, he hears no voice calling him to account for his actions, or, if he does hear a voice, feels no need to respond.

In less sophisticated natures, this presence of the others is projected also into the weapons and instruments of war. They become personalized, and the soldier becomes attached to them as an extension of himself. They afford him a vast comfort in difficult positions as a protection and a shield, a second skin. On the one hand, these weapons help to prevent the soldier from feeling responsible for the lives he takes. "I did not kill, my gun or grenade did it" is the subconscious suggestion. On the other hand, guns help to fill the intermediate spaces between him and the others. They help to cement the wall of comradeship that encloses him and ties him to his own side while at the same time preventing the enemy from becoming too real. Unless he is caught up in murderous ecstasy, destroying is easier when done at a little remove. With every foot of distance there is a corresponding decrease in reality. Imagination flags and fails altogether when distances become too great. So it is that much of the mindless cruelty of recent wars has been perpetrated by warriors at a distance, who could not guess what havoc their powerful weapons were occasioning.

Where weapons and comrades are insufficient to dampen self-awareness and personal responsibility, the soldier can often draw aid and comfort from the earth itself. His relation to nature is likely to be quite different from that elemental sense of belonging, which can also arouse in the perceptive person the most poetic and blissful feelings. The combat soldier hugs earth and trees as protection, as "cover" in the expressive military phrase. He does not now think of nature as the source of his life, but as his possible means of preserving it against those who would isolate and destroy him. Nature is part of his situation; it, too, is a presence in the special way that his weapons and his buddies are. If earth becomes dear, for example, the walls of his foxhole, trees, breastworks, clouds, and sun, it is not as part of nature that these things are dear. They are dear as instruments that shield him from the enemy. Everything is there for him, as it were, and yet he is there only for the others. He makes everything into an instrument, himself included. He is a trigger finger, a tank driver, a bombardier, a scout, and he can take delight in being an instrument. So everything conspires to prevent his coming to himself, and, as often as not, the soldier is a semiconscious accomplice in it as well. Why should he undergo the pain of reflection, the dangerous isolation acute self-awareness can bring with it?

In highly mechanized armies, many a soldier gains a certain fulfillment in serving the machine with which he is entrusted. The automatism of military life has been immeasurably increased by the perfection and intricacy of instruments and weapons, and it is certain that the human beings who serve them are actually influenced by their automatic character. Combat soldiers must adjust themselves to the laws of these mechanisms, and their habits become of necessity more and more mechanized. Individuality is inevitably suppressed when a group of soldiers have to co-ordinate their movements and all their daily activities in the proper functioning of an instrument of war. But the significant thing is that so many take pleasure in it. There is, I suppose, a perverse kind of freedom here, the freedom from reacting in novel and unpredictable ways. Whatever the source, love for the machine—and the more complicated and exacting, often the greater the love—is an important element in modern combat. The hardened German tanker cited earlier who broke down and cried at the loss of his tank is far from an isolated instance. Those thinkers who believe that a new type of man is bound to emerge as a product of our technological development might well study in detail over the last century the varying relation of men to their weapons of war.

In totalitarian countries, this willingness to become a functionary is much further developed because it is consciously pursued by the dictator at the summit. Self-awareness is fought as an enemy of communal enthusiasms. In 1944 and 1945 I had to listen to Fascist and Nazi police and party functionaries exclaim with nauseating regularity when they were captured: "My conscience is clear!" It made no difference how heinous the deeds were in which they had taken part, always the refrain was the same: "I have done nothing wrong. My conscience is clear." Despite early suspicions that these protestations masked real guilt feelings, I became convinced in the end that most of these men knew no genuine regrets for what they had done. As functionaries, guilt was for them, in any case, an empty word. If their consciences had ever awakened, the lack of response had long since silenced the call. The inhumanity that so appalled me about them was more often than not a kind of absence of feeling rather than sadistic perversion. Machines cannot respond; they can only perform, being at the service of something or someone else.

It was peculiarly abhorrent to me that these people expected the same treatment at my hands that they had meted out to their victims. One particularly repulsive officer of the Security Service, nicknamed "Genickschuss" from his reputation for shooting Polish underground fighters and hapless Jews in the back of the neck, hastily wrote a farewell note to his wife and children after I had interrogated him and consigned him to a jail cell. The jailer brought me his letter within the hour, asking me what to do with it. When I had read it, I was puzzled by the references to his imminent death.

"Does he mean to commit suicide?" I asked the German jailer.

He looked incredulous and answered simply, "Not a chance. He expects you to treat him as he treated his prisoners."

In a kind of baffled rage at the thought of his fearful crimes, I cried out, "And if I did what was right, that is just exactly what I should do."

I shall never forget the jailer's quiet reply. "Sir, it is necessary," he said.

For many soldiers, however, a much more conscious escape from responding to conscience is the fact that they are acting "under orders." Their superiors who issue the orders must take the blame and bear the consequences. When one asked, as I did, which superiors would bear responsibility, the answer was usually vague. Pressed far enough, it usually turned out to be the commander in chief who was to carry all the weight of guilt for deeds that, if committed in peacetime, would have brought heavy penalties.

I was amazed how many American civilian soldiers appeared to put great weight on taking the oath of the soldier. Frequently, I heard the remark: "When I raised my right hand and took that oath, I freed myself of the consequences for what I do. I'll do what they tell me and nobody can blame me." Of course, in a legal sense it is and has been customary in military organizations to hold the highest ranking officer responsible for deeds of his men committed under orders. But Anglo-Saxon lands have long since learned to distinguish between legal and moral responsibility, at least in peacetime. It was clear, however, that most of the soldiers who cited the oath felt that the moral responsibility was being shifted as well. The satisfaction in thus sloughing off responsibility was often plainly visible. Becoming a soldier was like escaping from one's own shadow. To commit deeds of violence without the usual consequences that society visits upon the violent seemed at first a bit unnatural but for many not unpleasant. All too quickly it could become a habit.

In a more legalistic nation like Germany, where the distinction between law and right or between state justice and private morality has never been sharply drawn, the abrogation of personal responsibility for one's deeds is even less complicated. It is hard for civilian America to comprehend the mental and moral conversion involved for a professional German soldier to oppose in full consciousness a military command. To most of us, it sounded like an easy excuse when Hitler's officers protested at Nuremberg and elsewhere that they were "carrying out orders" when they committed atrocities. To most of them, however, this was a sufficient explanation and excuse for their deeds. I suspect that the majority of Germans remain unconvinced that any soldier should be legally punished for "doing his duty," regardless of its inhumane character. I hardly need to add that many Americans, both professional military men and others, are also unpersuaded.

To be sure, since the Nuremberg trials, Western nations have officially denied the soldier's right to obey orders that involve him in crimes. He must distinguish between illegitimate orders and those that are in line with his duty as a soldier. Presumably, the distinction is always clear according to official pronouncements, but in reality under the conditions of total war few things are more difficult to distinguish. Our age is caught in a painful contradiction for which there is no resolution other than the renunciation of wars or at least of the way we have been waging them in this generation. On the other hand, we have come to believe in total victory over the foe, with the use of every means thinkable to effect this goal. Since the opponent's residual strength rests in his industrial potential and civilian labor force, we have found it necessary to disregard the age-old distinction between combatant and noncombatant. In these wars moral considerations become, as a consequence, increasingly irrelevant while the war is in progress. The longer they last the more nearly do the opposing sides approach that boundary where everything is allowed.

However, once the question of victory is decided, we are shocked beyond measure at such moral license and require stern punishment of the vanquished for violations of the rules of war. When reason gains some ascendancy over passion at the end of a war, nearly everyone can see that to turn over individual rights to desperate men, intent on victory at whatever cost, is to invite moral chaos. It seems that the more we transgress in recent wars upon everything essential to individual dignity, the more convinced we become afterward of the necessity of maintaining individual rights inviolate. Small wonder, however, that the majority of soldiers, dimly conscious of this contradiction, refuse to involve themselves in issues so confused and troubling.

Not at all certain whether they will later be considered by their own people as heroes or as scoundrels, great numbers find it simpler to ignore the moral problems by thinking of them as little as possible. Better to let the conscience sleep, to do as the others are doing and as one is told to do, and the future will bring what it will. Who knows whether there will be a future anyway? Most soldiers in wartime feel caught in the present so completely that they surrender their wills to their superiors and exist in the comforting anonymity of the crowd.

Though the above may be a correct, external description of the response or lack of response on the part of most soldiers to individual guilt in waging war, it nevertheless misses all the subtle ways in which guilt is incurred in conflict and made present to the conscience of the minority. There are degrees and kinds of guilt, and not merely a formal declaration of simple guilt or innocence by the inner tribunal. Those soldiers who do respond to the call of conscience find themselves involved in the most baffling situations, in which any action they could take is inappropriate. They learn soon that nearly any of the individual's relations to the world about him can involve him in guilt of some kind, particularly in warfare. It is as pervasive in life and reflection as is human freedom itself. Awakened to his personal responsibility in one aspect of combat action, the soldier is not necessarily awakened to finer nuances of guilt. Yet it sometimes happens that the awakening is thorough and absolute in character, demanding of the subject an entirely different set of relations to friend and enemy.

It is a crucial moment in a soldier's life when he is ordered to perform a deed that he finds completely at variance with his own notions of right and good. Probably for the first time, he discovers that an act someone else thinks to be necessary is for him criminal. His whole being rouses itself in protest, and he may well be forced to choose in this moment of awareness of his freedom an act involving his own life or death. He feels himself caught in a situation that he is powerless to change yet cannot himself be part of. The past cannot be undone and the present is inescapable. His only choice is to alter himself, since all external features are unchangeable.

What this means in the midst of battle can only inadequately be imagined by those who have not experienced it themselves. It means to set oneself against others and with one stroke lose their comforting presence. It means to cut oneself free of doing what one's superiors approve, free of being an integral part of the military organism with the expansion of the ego that such belonging brings. Suddenly the soldier feels himself abandoned and cast off from all security. Conscience has isolated him, and its voice is a warning. If you do this, you will not be at peace with me in the future. You can do it, but you ought not. You must act as a man and not as an instrument of another's will.

I shall always remember the face of a German soldier when he described such a drastic awakening as this. At the time we picked him up for investigation in the Vosges in 1944, he was fighting with the French Maquis against his own people. To my question concerning his motives for deserting to the French Resistance, he responded by describing his earlier involvement in German reprisal raids against the French. On one such raid, his unit was ordered to burn a village and to allow none of the villagers to escape. (Possibly the village was Oradour and the soldier was one of the participants in that grisly atrocity; at that time we knew little of what was happening elsewhere and I did not ask him for names.) As he told how women and children were shot as they fled screaming from the flames of their burning homes, the soldier's face was contorted in painful fashion and he was nearly unable to breathe. It was quite clear that this extreme experience had shocked him into full awareness of his own guilt, a guilt he feared he would never atone. At the moment of that awakening he did not have the courage or resolution to hinder the massacre, but his desertion to the Resistance soon after was evidence of a radically new course. Terrible as was his self-reproach at what now could not be undone, he had won himself through this experience and would never again be available as a functionary.

In the Netherlands, the Dutch tell of a German soldier who was a member of an execution squad ordered to shoot innocent hostages. Suddenly he stepped out of rank and refused to participate in the execution. On the spot he was charged with treason by the officer in charge and was placed with the hostages, where he was promptly executed by his comrades. In such an act the soldier has abandoned once and for all the security of the group and exposed himself to the ultimate demands of freedom. He responded in the crucial moment to the voice of conscience and was no longer driven by external commands. In this case we can only guess what must have been the influence of his deed on slayers and slain. At all events, it was surely not slight, and his example on those who hear of the episode cannot fail to be inspiriting. Were it not for the revelation of nobility in mankind, which again and again appears in time of war, we could scarcely endure reading the literature of combat.

These are, of course, extreme examples and not to be taken as typical. Normally, the awakening of guilt is much more gradual, and the achievement of clarity about duty to one's country and duty to oneself a matter of anguished doubt, sometimes lasting for months or years. But the primary realization is the same in all cases: there is a line that a man dare not cross, deeds he dare not commit, regardless of orders and the hopelessness of the situation, for such deeds would destroy something in him that he values more than life itself. He may decide that his commander, his army, or his people may justly demand his life but may not command him to do what is in violation of his deepest self. However clear he may be about this momentous conclusion in moments of quiet and repose, the soldier is not thereby steeled against anxiety and fear of death. In the melee of conflict he may at times feel as do his unawakened comrades, that life is all he has, after all. Personal resolution is constantly attacked by the strain and disorder of combat life. His body, he discovers, is not always subject to his will. Impulses and emotions sweep him away, causing him to act again and again contrary to his sense of right. Against his innermost desire, he involves himself in guilt. Conscience within him is a voice long before it is a power; he desires to respond long before he has the required resolution. Though the voice is insistent, more clamorous impulses are able to dominate him in moments of violent action.

Nevertheless, his conscience has established an image of the ideal, a man who will acquit himself in whatever situation with independence and dignity. His inner history henceforth in combat will be the struggle to live up to this ideal. It may be that the soldier is contending against fear that he will involuntarily desert his comrades in a critical moment and be responsible for their death. It may be that he has qualms against killing enemy soldiers. Or he may be utterly persuaded of the justice of his country's cause and of the necessity of destroying lives to realize that cause, yet strongly opposed to this or that means his side is employing. He may be struggling to acquit himself well in a tangle of personal relationships common to military organizations in times of tension and peril. The occasions and situations are manifold in which the soldier who can no longer pass responsibility for his acts to others must struggle to gain full possession of himself. The voice of conscience is forever convicting him of inadequacy and insufficiency, urging him to better efforts. The ideal of acquitting himself like a man comes to appear utopian when he is confronted with certain situations.

Guilt is likely to come upon him in many other ways than as a consequence of natural fear of pain or death. Modern wars are full of border situations where a soldier is forced to choose between evils and where every choice is like leaping into the dark because its consequences are unforeseeable. Rarely will

187

he find a situation as clearly wrong as the shooting of hostages
or the strafing of fleeing civilians. On the contrary, he will
often have to choose between helping a wounded comrade to
safety or remaining at his post to protect others whom he does
not know. Sometimes he will have to choose the welfare of his
unit at the expense of other units or the civilian populace.
Hunger and cold and animal needs are everywhere in war in
the midst of superfluity of food and warmth and delicacies.
When he gives up his food or warm room in favor of some
pitiful urchin or haggard mother, such charity can hardly
comfort him because it is so transient. In the face of the need,
his efforts will seem inconsequential to the point of futility.
Even though the soldier may become a relatively selfless man
in the service of the civil populace and his weaker comrades,
he will seldom be at ease with himself. In some degree he will
feel guilty of omitting to do what he ought, or doing what he
ought not. This is inevitable, of course, for he is an individual
who thinks of himself and others as ends in themselves in a
situation where human beings are means for superpersonal
goals. Men are materials to be expended for national interests,
real or imagined. All the awakened soldier can hope to do in
such a society is to meliorate the lot of the less fortunate, to
act in an inhumane environment as humanely as possible.
Opportunities to be humane are ordinarily plentiful enough
in combat zones, but his freedom is constricted on all sides. It
is like moving on a rack.

Such a soldier is likely to suffer most of all from the commands of military superiors when they are close to the border
zone of the forbidden, that is, when they transgress the line
that he cannot cross if he is to live with his conscience. The
satisfaction that the unawakened conscience takes in making
itself an instrument of higher wills is for the awakened con-

science a leading source of its misery. To be required to carry out orders in which he does not believe, given by men who are frequently far removed from the realities with which the orders deal and often motivated by abstract hatred—this is the familiar lot of the combat soldier. The man of conscience can survive morally only by following the letter of such orders and disobeying their intention.

It is a great boon of front-line positions that this disobedience is frequently possible, since supervision is not very exact where danger of death is present. Many a conscientious soldier has discovered he could reinterpret military orders in his own spirit before obeying them. The fortunate ones have escaped difficulties with their commanders; the unfortunate have often ended in disciplinary barracks or even a death cell. At all events, the tension in such a soldier between the voice of conscience and the demands made upon him as a means and instrument of higher authority will rarely relax. The alternatives to this tension are for him either the surrender of his conscience to superiors or open defiance of their orders with fateful consequences to his life and freedom. Both alternatives he will seek to avoid as long as possible.

Here is a personal example. For several months in World War II, I was attached to an infantry division whose divisional intelligence officer, a colonel, was an insensitive military tyrant. He was pleased to have our detachment of six men under his control and at the same time was deeply resentful of our superior educational backgrounds and independence of mind. He liked to meddle with our somewhat specialized job of interrogating the civilian populace in the search for spies and saboteurs the retreating Germans might have left behind or sent over the front. Increasingly, I found myself resenting and resisting his often harsh orders for civilian restrictions and prohibitions. As linguists, we were his only means of communication with the civilian populace, who were regarded by him as an infernal nuisance to be tolerated only because they could not be conveniently expelled from combat areas.

When our division entered the first towns of Alsace, we encountered numerous young Alsatians in civilian clothes who had deserted from the German armies when on furlough and hidden out at the risk of their lives while awaiting our advance. The Alsatians had helped to hide these youths from the ruthless clutches of the Gestapo. Some of them had previously served with the French against the Germans, but when Alsace and Lorraine were incorporated in Germany with the defeat of France in 1940, they had been conscripted into Hitler's armies, only to desert at the first opportunity. There was, of course, much rejoicing now that they could at last leave their hiding places and greet old friends and neighbors publicly once more. Many of them came to us and offered their help in intelligence work. Hard pressed as we were for help (only two in our detachment knew German well enough to be effective), we found much for them to do.

But the colonel had noticed the appearance of young men on the streets here in contrast to France, where male youth had been conspicuously absent. He called our detachment commander by telephone and demanded an explanation. With our briefing, the captain gave him the facts of the situation. The colonel's response was immediate: "Do they have discharge papers from the German Army?" It was explained to him that deserters were never supplied with discharge papers, that being contrary to the usage of the German Army. His conclusion was breath-taking. In that case, these men were prisoners of war, and we were to round them up and ship them in prisoner trucks through regular channels to the huge camps in France. The colonel insisted on quick action. Our captain, who was sympathetic with us but afraid of the colonel, begged us to arrest the deserters the next day as ordered.

I was fortunate in having as a German-speaking colleague a strong-minded and intelligent young man of Boston Irish descent. He was profane, not overly scrupulous on moral issues, but fair-minded. He and I determined not to obey the order. To obey it would be the one way to alienate completely this friendly and much-mistreated Alsatian people. For parents to see their sons, who had risked their lives escaping from the German Army, loaded on the same trucks with hated German soldiers and transported to prison camps would be to embitter relations with their "liberators" from the beginning. Moreover, the orders were manifestly unjust to these young men, who felt themselves to be allies and wanted in every way to aid our cause. The two of us hoped to avoid the issue by simply ignoring the order and continuing our other work, of which we had more than enough. But the colonel called again and was this time insulting and insistent. Still we ignored him, though our captain begged us to act. The third day, the colonel was threatening us with court-martial and worse for disobeying a direct order.

What were we to do? The two of us talked it over and decided to continue to refuse. It was not so much courage on my part as physical weariness and moral disgust at the injustices of warfare. In the most obscene language, my associate declared that the Army could court-martial him a hundred times and he would not obey such a stupid, senseless command. His mood was one of weary, sullen resistance to the vast stupidity of higher headquarters. He had been much longer in the war than I, having served with distinction in Africa and

Sicily as well as in Italy and France. If his concern with the injustice of the order was not as great as mine, his resoluteness was greater, and fortified me. I had visions of the forbidding disciplinary barracks we had glimpsed in North Africa, of a dishonorable discharge and the disgrace it would bring on my aged father, who would not be able to understand why I had to disobey. Still, I knew that if I did not draw the line here I would be unable to draw it anywhere. If I did not refuse to become a party to the arrest of innocent, wronged men, I could not refuse to do anything that this or any other colonel ordered. I felt myself to be at the end of a tether. This was to be a showdown, and I had little doubt as to the winner. The loneliness and isolation of spirit that swept over me served to teach me how much I had hitherto been sustained by the silent approval of "the others." Even my partner in disobedience could not lift from me the heavy spiritual burden, for he was bitter and cynical about the whole affair.

Fortunately, things turned out in very different fashion from the expected. The colonel decided to call up army headquarters and report our insubordination before taking further action. He chanced to reach an intelligent officer who knew us both slightly, and this officer wanted to know why we persisted in disobeying orders. This the colonel had never stopped to determine, but when he did communicate the cause, Army Intelligence found our reasons good and within a day or two sent through an order that all Alsatian deserters were to be left with their families and in no case to be transported anywhere with German prisoners of war.

We had unexpectedly won the day and drew comfort afterward from the report that where our division had gone through Alsace the population was distinctly more pro-American than in other parts of Alsace-Lorraine. In areas where the deserters had been arrested, they had been forced to undergo manifold hardships and humiliations in prisoner-of-war camps, ironically enough because they were not in uniform, and were treated by our troops as cowardly and unworthy the respect accorded regular prisoners.

This was only an incident of war, not objectively important except as it influenced sectors of a population for or against the Allied cause. But subjectively it was for me a kind of turning point. As a result of it, I gained no great confidence in my ability to withstand extreme pressures from official authority, yet I had determined that a line could be drawn between personal rights and military demands. Though I knew that sheer good fortune had prevented the normal consequences of disobedience from falling upon me, I felt, nevertheless, immensely strengthened for a possible second refusal. More important, the incident cleared my mind on the vexed question of the relation of the individual to his state. Hard as they were to assert, I now felt convinced that the individual had his absolute rights even in the desperate struggle for survival that is modern war. And survival without integrity of conscience is worse than perishing outright, or so it seemed to me. Nothing had furthered my self-knowledge so much since my encounter with the old man of the mountain in Italy the year before.

I have no doubt that many others have found themselves in much more crucial difficulties in warfare than this example illustrates. Yet, curiously enough, most contemporary war novels deal with nearly every agony of combat except this one. Where matters of conscience are taken up, as in the immensely popular *Caine Mutiny*, there is frequently an ambivalence in the attitude of the author toward the rights of conscience against military organization. In Wouk's novel, for instance, the reader is left in doubt about the moral justification for "the mutiny," despite the fact that the captain of the *Caine* is portrayed in the worst possible light. He is cowardly, completely neurotic, a pathological liar, and incapable of giving orders that will save his ship from destruction. Yet, the author reminds us, he is a commander in the United States Navy, of long service, and as such an early fighter against the evil enemies of his country. Perhaps he should be obeyed despite his incapacity, since the principles of obedience and discipline count for more in a war of survival than individual conscience and private morality. This is typical of the modern confusion about the spheres of individual right and state authority in the era of total war.

However, the man of awakened conscience actually caught in this dilemma, as contrasted with the author writing a book about it, will usually be clear that duty to himself prohibits him from acting contrary to his voice, regardless of his fears and the personal consequences. He may obey such orders, but at the cost of his moral integrity. The safe observer has no right to blame him, for the sternest self-discipline is demanded. Few men in any age have had the moral stamina of a Socrates, who many centuries ago decided for himself that it was a right and duty to disobey his state and people when he felt they were wrong, but not his right to flee from their punishment for that disobedience. If few young men can be expected to attain the resolution of a mature Socrates, the reflective soldier is nearly certain to share the Socratic trust in the reliability of his conscience when it is in conflict with the group will.

This is particularly true of the conscience that is supported by faith in its divine origin. A secure religious faith has enabled many a soldier to act in defiance of unjust commands or to overcome the temptation to save himself at the cost of others. As I have pointed out elsewhere, the testimony of those condemned officers and soldiers who struck against Hitler in 1944 is eloquent and instructive evidence of this fact. Judging from their last letters to friends and family members, not all of them had religious support for their consciences. Those who had no religious faith or hope for life after death acted as courageously as the others and faced the end with confidence in the justice of their cause. Nevertheless, their sadness stands in sharp contrast with the tranquillity and even exaltation of those who were believers. Both groups seemed immensely relieved to be freed from the pressure of conformity to a system and a party they had learned to despise. The difference between them was that those of religious faith took leave of their lives as though the physical end was the beginning of something mysterious yet marvelous.

There is a kind of guilt that transcends the personal responsibility of the sensitive conscience and burdens that soldier particularly who retains faith in the cause and the country for which he is fighting. It is the guilt the individual shares as a member of a military unit, a national fighting force, a people at war. We may call it social or political or collective guilt; it is not essentially different for the civilian than for the soldier, and it is inescapable. No matter how self-contained and isolated in spirit the man of conscience may feel, he cannot avoid the realization that he is a participant in a system and an enterprise whose very essence is violence and whose spirit is to win at whatever cost. For the soldier, it is his squad or company or division that performs deeds abhorrent to him. No matter how strongly he abjures personal responsibility for this or that deed, he cannot escape social responsibility. So long as he wears the same uniform as his fellows, he will be regarded by outsiders as one of them. His fellows, too, treat him as a member of the fraternity of men at arms. The conscience within him may be more and more appalled by the heedlessness of group behavior and the mechanical ruthlessness of an organization whose dedication to violence gives it an unholy character. I was appalled and yet I could not escape it. I wrote in my journal one day at the height of the war:

Yesterday we caught two spies, making our recent total five. We are getting a reputation as a crack detachment. One had to be severely beaten before he confessed. It was pretty horrible, and I kept away from the room where it was done ... though I could not escape his cries of pain. . . . I lay awake until three o'clock this morning. . . . I thought of the Hamlet line as most appropriate, "Tis bitter cold and I am sick at heart."

A soldier with an awakened conscience who is a member of such a community, coarse, vulgar, heedless, violent, realizes with overpowering clarity the possibility of being alienated from his own kind. This uniformed, machine-like monster, the combat unit, drives him back into himself and repels him utterly. Toward individuals who make it up, he can gain many relationships, but the collectivity itself chokes him without mercy.

Toward his nation as a nation he may well come to experience in his innermost self the same lack of relationship. A state at war reveals itself to the penetrating eye in its clearest light and the spectacle is not beautiful. Nietzsche's likeness of it to a cold snake is, from one perspective, not greatly exaggerated. The awakened conscience will recognize a part of this spirit of the nation in the hate-filled speeches of politician-patriots, in the antipathy toward dissenting opinions about the utter virtue of its cause, in the ruthlessness with which the individual is sacrificed for real or alleged national advantages. It will despise the fanaticism with which this state makes morally dubious and historically relative ends into absolutes, its perversity in maintaining pride at whatever price in human misery.

At the same time, justice will force this soldier to admit that these are his people, driven by fear and hatred, who are directing this vast mechanism. If he is honest with himself he will admit that he, too, is a violent man on occasion and capable of enjoying the fruits of violence. Legally, and more than legally, he belongs to the community of soldiers and to the state. At some level of his being he can understand why they perform as they do and can find it in his heart to feel sorry for some of the politicians and higher officers. In their place he wonders if he would do any better than they. He is bound to reflect that his nation has given him refuge and sustenance, provided him whatever education and property he calls his own. He belongs and will always belong to it in some sense, no matter where he goes or how hard he seeks to alter his inheritance. The crimes, therefore, that his nation or one of its units commits cannot be indifferent to him. He shares the guilt as he shares the satisfaction in the generous deeds and worthy products of nation or army. Even if he did not consciously will them and was unable to prevent them, he cannot wholly escape responsibility for collective deeds.

He belongs and yet he does not belong. "I did not ask to be born," he is likely to tell himself while struggling with his responsibility for collective deeds, "and I did not choose my nation. Had I been given a choice of places to grow up at various stages in my education I might have chosen other than the nation in which I was accidentally born. I am, of course, a citizen of this nation and am willing to expose my life in its defense. But in my inner being I belong only to the community that I have freely chosen, my friends, my club, my church, my profession. All other associations of mine are external and accidental, however little I may have realized it earlier. This does not free me from the guilt that this nation is heaping upon itself, so long as I participate in its defense. I shall always be guilty as long as I belong to a nation at all. Yet there is no good life apart from some nation or other."

It is clear to him that his political guilt is of a different sort from the personal, since the latter stems from his freedom in a direct way, the former only in part. The nation was in being long before him and will presumably continue in being after his death. Hence his capacity to change its course is immeasurably limited by its history as well as by his own powers. For the politically conscious soldier, this does not mean, however, that it is negligible. Insofar as his political guilt is in direct relation to his freedom, he will become conscious of what he has done or failed to do to promote or hinder the humanizing of military or political means and objectives. He will be certain at all events that he has not done enough. On this or that occasion he has been silent when he should have spoken out. In his own smaller or larger circle of influence he has not made his whole weight felt. Had he brought forth the civil courage to protest in time, some particular act of injustice might have been avoided. Whatever the level of influence the soldier commands, from the squad or platoon to the command of armies, in some manner he is able to affect the course of group action.

When the nation for which he is fighting has enjoyed a free government and been previously responsive to its citizens' wishes, he will be conscious of greater responsibility than will the soldier whose government is authoritarian or totalitarian.

The greater the possibility of free action in the communal sphere, the greater the degree of guilt for evil deeds done in the name of everyone. Still, the degrees of guilt are impossible to assess for anyone else, and hardly any two people share an equal burden of communal guilt. The soldier may have been too young as a civilian to have exerted much influence on events or he may have been too poorly informed or confused to know where his political duty lay. As a soldier, he may be in too isolated or insignificant a location to make effective use of his freedom. No citizen of a free land can justly accuse his neighbor, I believe, of political guilt, of not having done as much as he should to prevent the state of war or the commission of this or that state crime. But each can—and the man of conscience will—accuse himself in proportion to the freedom he had to alter the course of events.

The peculiar agony of the combat soldier's situation is that, even more than in his struggle with his own ideal self, he is aware of the puniness of his individual powers to effect a change. War not only narrows the limits of personal freedom, but it likewise constricts the individual's communal liberty, his capacity to make his power felt in significant ways. The sense of impotence will weigh upon him day after day. Though the man of awakened conscience will hardly believe that the war is a natural catastrophe, he will not know how any individual can alter its seemingly inexorable course. Personal guilt can be in some measure atoned and the struggle to improve can be taken up every morning anew. But communal guilt comes upon him in ever increasing measure in any war, and he is likely to feel utterly inadequate either to atone for it or prevent its accumulation.

For instance, when the news of the atomic bombing of Hiroshima and Nagasaki came, many an American soldier felt shocked and ashamed. The combat soldier knew better than did Americans at home what those bombs meant in suffering and injustice. The man of conscience wherever he was realized intuitively that the vast majority of the Japanese in both cities were no more, if no less, guilty of the war than were his own parents, sisters, or brothers. In his shame, he may have said to himself, as some of us did: "The next atomic bomb, dropped in anger, will probably fall on my own country and we will have deserved it." Such a conviction will hardly relieve him of the heavy sense of wrong that his nation committed and the responsibility for which he must now in some measure share. All the arguments used in justification—the shortening of the war by many months and the thousands of American lives presumably saved—cannot alter the fact that his government was the first to use on undefended cities, without any warning, a monstrous new weapon of annihilation.

Worst of all about such deeds is that millions accepted and felt relief. Hearing this near-exultation in the enemy's annihilation, one can only conclude that political guilt has another source than the freedom of the individual to affect group action. It lies in the degree of his identification with the goals and the means of realizing them that his nation adopts. The person who inwardly approves an immoral action of his government or military unit testifies to his own probable decision had he possessed the freedom and opportunity of the actors. Freedom is possible, therefore, not only in the power to do or prevent, but also in inner assent and consent to action by others. With a relative criterion like this it is, of course, impossible to be exact in estimating even one's own guilt. Yet the jubilation in evil deeds allows little room for doubt that inner consent is often forthcoming. So do thousands of people increase their political guilt in wartime beyond the range of their direct action.

To some extent after World War I and explicitly after World War II, doctrines of collective guilt have become common. The German nation, for example, and particularly the German Army is often said to be guilty for having fought for Hitler in his aggressive wars of conquest and rapine. However innocent the individual soldier may have been of any personal misconduct, the fact that he was a member of a criminal conspiracy to deprive other peoples of their independence by violent means made him guilty. What justice is there in such a claim? To what extent is a German soldier in the last war guilty who kept himself free of personal crimes but was forced to experience, more or less directly, atrocities committed by his fellow soldiers and who was not blind to Hitler's mad ambitions? Is he not in an utterly different position from the soldier of a nation like ours who fought the war defensively to repel aggression?

In terms of what I have previously said, the answer can only be that no outsider has a moral right to make such an accusation about either the soldiery or the people as a whole. For an anti-Nazi soldier to have interfered with some act of injustice carried out by his fellow countrymen would have resulted in his prompt execution, as enough recorded instances prove. Apart from the demands of courage and determination that such an act requires, the question that tormented some soldiers in this situation was: What political purpose will my sacrifice serve? Many a conscientious German soldier might have screwed up his courage to open interference had he seen clearly in what way his death would have helped prevent further crimes. Fortunate soldiers found the right moment and the right deed with which to strike against the system they despised, and their chance to witness made them content to die. Others fought to the end of the war without such opportunities or without the necessary courage. Only those who sacrificed themselves in similar situations have the right to accuse them, and probably few of them would care to do so, if they were alive and able. For my own deeds I am responsible and can be held accountable, even if I act under the orders of another. For the deeds of my fellow men, specifically my fellow countrymen, my responsibility cannot be a public or legal one, for it is too dependent on my estimate of my ability to hinder criminal acts and of my inner consent to their commission.

Yet if accusations of collective guilt are unjustified, the sensitive German soldier could hardly escape the consciousness of his own political guilt. A burning sense of shame at the deeds of his government and the acts of horror committed by German soldiers and police was the mark of a conscientious German at the close of the war. "I am ashamed to be a German" was a not infrequent remark when friend was speaking to friend as the revelations of what the Third Reich had done became generally known. To be sure, those without conscience considered that they had atoned sufficiently for their political "mistakes" by their suffering during and after the war, and rejected with indignation any imputation of collective guilt. They wanted to hear nothing of their vicarious part in the crimes of their fellow citizens.

The reflective man knows in his heart what rarely crosses his lips, that the sins of his fellows are not so remote from him as he would like. If he is a soldier, he, too, has yielded at times to the temptations of power and the license that violence evokes in all of us. However free he may have kept himself from external participation in evil deeds and however foreign cruelty may be to his better nature, he will be aware that there

202

is in nearly all men the capacity for criminal deeds and the obscure yearning for license to act without consequences, hence his recognition of the chains of communal responsibility and his knowledge that atonement in this sphere is largely chimerical. No human power could atone for the injustice, suffering, and degradation of spirit of a single day of warfare. All of us shared the guilt, as I wrote in my journal on two occasions.

I talked yesterday to a young Viennese deserter . . . he had had nothing to eat but potato soup. . . . The picture he gave of the prison was grim enough. . . . One man, suspected of being a spy, was given nothing to eat for six days and was now past hunger. If he talked he would be shot as a spy, if he didn't he would starve —a difficult choice. The youth was strong, courteous. . . . He finally asked me in German, "Do I have to go back to Epinal?" And his whole soul was in the question and in his eyes. I said no, that was all past for him, and his face was suddenly illumined. I felt in a moment the whole stark tragedy of this war. What bitter cruelty all of us exercise! We are guilty and deserve the extreme penalty. Nothing that happens to me in future will I ever feel unjust and unmerited.

This morning was spent in attempting to control the mass of refugees streaming around here, some 2000 in a town whose population hardly exceeds 5000. This fate is pathetic, and more and more this problem of displaced persons becomes tremendous. Germany was really a slave state on a gigantic scale. Almost all of these foreign workers are on the roads, a few hours after their liberation, going they know not where, but away from the front and toward home, they hope, though thousands must know that they have no longer a home. But this afternoon Seitz and I saw something ten times worse. There was a concentration camp not far from here, and last Saturday the German guards loaded the inmates onto freight trains and tried to haul them away. When they discovered that the trains could not proceed, they left them

near a town named Osterburken. We found them there this after-
noon, some 880, half-dead, horribly starved people, among them
300 French Maquis, political prisoners. . . . To see these living
deaths in their striped suits in rags, dragging their feet, was a
sight that I would have done without. To add to its gruesomeness,
there was a dead German soldier deserter, who had been hanged
and whose body was lying by the road under a tree. Someone
had cut him down but the rope was still around his neck and his
feet were tied. He had been an attractive youngster, and one could
pretty well guess his story. The SS who had hanged him will one
day have to pay, and those who were responsible for the unim-
aginable suffering of these concentration-camp inmates will pay
also.

The realization of political guilt is poignantly expressed in
a poem by Albrecht Haushofer, one of the determined and
long-standing opponents of Hitler, who was imprisoned and
finally executed near the end of the war. His little book of
poems entitled *Moabiter Sonette,* written in a Berlin prison
while his hands were shackled, testifies to political guilt of a
man who had already atoned more than is required of most of
us. In the sonnet entitled *Schuld* (Guilt), he begins by noting
how easy it is for him to carry the guilt that his Nazi court
trial wanted to load upon him. To them he was a traitor to his
people in the plot against Hitler. Then he concludes in the
German version, to which I have added a literal translation:

Doch schuldig bin ich anders als ihr denkt,
ich müsste früher meine Pflicht erkennen
ich müsste schärfer Unheil Unheil nennen—
mein Urteil hab ich viel zu lang gelenkt . . .

Ich klage mich in meinem Herzen an:
Ich habe mein Gewissen lang betrogen
Ich hab mich selbst und andere belogen—

ich kannte früh des Jammers ganze Bahn—
ich hab gewarnt—nicht hart genug und klar!
Und heute weiss ich, was ich schuldig war . . .

Yet I am guilty otherwise than you think.
I should have known my duty earlier
And called evil by its name more sharply—
My judgment I kept flexible too long . . .

In my heart I accuse myself of this:
I deceived my conscience long
I lied to myself and others—

Early I knew the whole course of this misery—
I warned—but not hard enough or clearly!
Today I know of what I am guilty . . .

Thus the conscientious German soldier may well feel greater political guilt than a conscientious Allied soldier, depending on the measure of assent he had given to the National Socialist regime and the freedom of action he possessed. But the quality of his political guilt will hardly be different, for the warfare was not carried on by angels against devils, but by soldiers in a relatively just cause fighting soldiers in a relatively unjust cause. If the character of Hitler and his paladins gave to the Allied side a moral justification unusual in warfare, the Western nations have no reason to forget their share of responsibility for Hitler's coming to power or their dubious common cause with the Russian dictator. The reflective soldier on both sides of the conflict will see no escape from political guilt as long as he remains a member of a state. If, in his disillusionment, he is tempted to renounce his nation and pledge his allegiance to the human race alone, this, too, will prove illusory, for mankind collectively is doubtless as predisposed to injustice as nations are.
. . .

It is precisely this realization that may lead the soldier to a recognition that personal and political guilt are hardly resolvable on their own levels. They involve a guilt that can only be called metaphysical, because it concerns man's very being and its relations to the rest of the cosmos. The root of the guilt problem lies in human nature itself, in our failure as human beings to live in accordance with our potentialities and our vision of the good. Because we do fail, our spirits are isolated and closed to each other. None of us can be to another as we really desire to be, for we strike against something strange and alien in him. The sympathies of even the most reflective and sensitive do not extend far enough to overcome entirely the antipathy toward his fellows that is in nearly all of us. In some facet of our being we are closed and indifferent, not open to others or concerned with their fate. Though most of us are capable of feeling compassion for the suffering of men, and recognize our common kinship in isolation and loneliness, this recognition is rarely strong enough to influence our action decisively. We cannot love enough either our fellow men or our common mother, the nature from which we originate and to which we return. As human beings, we are in a perpetual state of disequilibrium with the rest of creation, neither humble enough to recognize our dependence nor bold enough to actualize our powers.

If this is capable of oppressing many of us in time of peace, it is easy to imagine with how much greater force it strikes a reflective soldier in combat. Everywhere he experiences himself and his comrades as violators of the earth. The ruthlessness with which organized warriors deal with the order of nature in order to defend their miserable lives will appall him, all the more so in modern times, when the scorched-earth policy has been succeeded by atomic destruction. The crimes against horses and other animals that men press into the service of their insane passions, the recklessness in destroying human habitations and works of art, full of the dignity and genius of human labor, will rob him forever of any exaggerated hope for the species. When his martial passions are kindled, this pygmy of creation is capable of defying the creative source of all life and flinging away all that he has formerly cherished. Like the ancient Titans of fable, he seems intent on storming the ramparts of heaven and calling down upon himself a novel kind of punishment.

Faced with this presumptuousness of the human creature, his closedness and dearth of love, the awakened soldier will be driven to say in his heart: "I, too, belong to this species. I am ashamed not only of my own deeds, not only of my nation's deeds, but of human deeds as well. I am ashamed to be a man." This is the culmination of a passionate logic which begins in warfare with the questioning of some act the soldier has been ordered to perform contrary to his conscience. Consciousness of failure to act in response to conscience can lead to the greatest revulsion, not only for oneself, but for the human species. How many soldiers have experienced in battle a profound distaste for the human creature! I wrote of my own despair:

It is eleven o'clock at night, and raining. The town is quiet, a fresh breeze, rain-laden, is blowing. I sit alone in my room and ponder my own limitations, wondering why the whole mystery of the universe must be closed, why I must plod on in the path of so many others, subject to the same temptations and weaknesses. Such nights as these have for years beaten in upon me my failures, my blindness, and the impenetrable nature of the world.

The combat soldier who experiences this guilt of the human creature deeply is likely to be caught in a serious inner crisis.

On the one hand, he perceives the degraded and degrading level of human life, as battle experiences can so well teach it. And this degradation does not seem to be a consequence of war conditions so much as war conditions are a consequence of it. His whole being rebels against this condition; his conscience warns him that it ought not to be. Neither he nor the others deserve to be spared. All are such caricatures of what they should be that death appears to be the only fitting resolution. On the other hand, he is plunged into doubt about the possibility of attaining to any other state. Perhaps men are what they are by virtue of some hidden necessity in the nature of things. Is it wise to expect anything else than the spectacle now offered? The despairing soldier seeks for a reason why men are the creatures they show themselves to be in combat, and the reason that has appealed over many generations is the idea of necessity. Freedom may be after all an illusion, and the conscience within me, always protesting, be fatally wrong.

This classic struggle between freedom and necessity often tears the heart of one who has advanced a little in the consciousness of guilt. Perhaps the feeling of necessity is the final refuge of that spirit in us which resists all attempts at self-reproach, that uncivilizable ego which stops at nothing to justify the self in its lowest, most aggressive manifestations. Or it may be simply the hopelessness of the effort to rid oneself of metaphysical guilt that makes belief in necessity so attractive. At any rate, for the soldier in battle, the arguments for necessity look very strong indeed. The voice of conscience can be so easily explained away in terms of childhood indoctrination and religious superstition. It is tempting to attack the validity of the feeling of freedom through its questionable origin.

Some survive this crisis of faith only by yielding up their

belief in the individual's responsibility for his actions. The moral cynics, which modern wars generate in great numbers, testify to a lost hope in mankind. Where cynicism is not mere shallowness and show, it is the cry of men who have not been able to endure the tension between their inner ideal and outer reality. They resolve not to take the world or themselves seriously any longer and give themselves over to enjoyment. But everyone notices that there is a pathos about their gaiety, and their frivolity is hardly contagious.

The soldier who does not succumb to the seductions of a theory of necessity, but attempts, instead, to resolve the conflict through reason finds himself long exposed to indecisive inner doubts. Gradually he may come to realize that neither freedom nor determinism can be established satisfactorily except in an emotional sense. In practice, it is not difficult to convince himself that he is free to change. On reflection, however, the clarity that practice generates searches the past and finds necessity, the other looks to action in present and future and asserts freedom. In serene moments the soldier may be very clear that he is partly free, in projecting himself into the future and striving for an ideal; partly determined, in being limited by what he has done and been. Yet whether his own freedom is not a tiny aspect of some larger necessity will escape his best efforts at analysis. At times he becomes convinced that the two are not opposed at all, but in a mysterious way two sides of the same coin.

The logic of most soldiers with a deep sense of guilt is a logic of passion, and all the subtleties of the problem will normally be lost on them. If at times such a soldier is too tired out or occupied with other cares to feel distressed in any way, the conflict is likely to be driven deeper into his unconscious mind, there to weigh on his spirit and foster melancholy. What

he longs for essentially is a simple piety, an attitude of grate-
fulness and acceptance for the created. He loses whatever
satisfaction he formerly took in the destructive ways of war.
Man as *Homo furens* appears now to be a monster to him,
for this soldier has learned to cherish solely the human function as preserver and conserver of created things.

Many a soldier in this predicament has found a blessed
release in the certainty that there is a higher order of reality
where the irresolvable is resolved. It can be—indeed, often
is—a rather primitive trust in the ultimate justice and mercy
of a heavenly father, in whom justice and mercy are not at
odds. In a sense, the surrender here is similar to the satisfaction in believing that necessity is ruler of all. But the difference
is apparent in the richness of meaning that religious trust
evidently brings. All previous struggles are seen to have been
necessary preparation and purification for present assurance.
In God all that appears endlessly difficult for human reason is
mysteriously purposeful and clear. Apart from the validity of
the religious resolution of guilt (and for the nonbeliever it
appears to be little more than an escape mechanism), the
efficacy of this path is beyond any other that mortal man has
found.

If the soldier possesses a primary religious nature, he can
derive absolution and exaltation from his capacity for repentance and surrender to the will of the divine. He loses any
need for death and sometimes, too, the fear of death as well,
for he has gained the great virtue of hope, which is perhaps
the strongest hold in life and is that virtue which is peculiar
to religion. If it does not free him from the usual troubles of
the flesh, religious hope does assure him that there is a realm
on the other side of human weakness and guilt. His one desire
is to act in accord with his hope in this supreme reality, and,

if he is a Christian, the prayer that will be most often on his lips is: Not my will but Thine be done. Personal and political guilt, which may have weighed upon him unendurably before, are now resolved in this childlike trust in a single interpretation and interpreter.

For the more philosophical temperament, however, there is no immediate solution or resolution to metaphysical guilt. If such a soldier is strong enough, the insight gained through his recognition of this most comprehensive form of guilt may help him gradually win a new relationship to his fellows and to the cosmos. Guilt can teach him, as few things else are able to, how utterly a man can be alienated from the very sources of his being. But the recognition may point the way to a reunion and a reconciliation with the varied forms of the created. In short, he may pass beyond his rejection of the human species and gain a new grasp of his world. Such a soldier will discover his future mission in life to be as far removed as possible from the destructive work of war. He will be absorbed in the reconstructive, the simple, and the truly humane arts. Atonement will become for him not an act of faith or a deed, but a life, a life devoted to strengthening the bonds between men and between man and nature. He will not be in any obvious way a reformer or a social worker or a preacher. But among his friends he will be known as extraordinarily gentle, sane, and wise.

These are some of the outcomes of a metaphysical conviction of guilt. Some it can drive mad; some to the barely covert wish for death. Others are overwhelmed by the belief that all is necessary, and conclude very often that nothing really matters except pleasures of the senses. Still others triumph through religious faith or through a philosophical reconciliation with man and nature, thus using guilt as a means to a firmer and

211

more enduring hold on life. Metaphysical guilt may well be as prevalent in peace as in war, since all men incur it to greater or lesser extent. Frequently, however, it necessitates an excess of moral and political guilt to force our acceptance of this reality. In this sphere, too, some men require the utter exposure and extreme experiences of combat to come to their true selves.

I find it hard to believe that in the wars of our day any great number of soldiers attain the possibilities that lie in the acceptance of guilt. As I indicated earlier, the reasons appear to lie in a dominant mood of our times and in the different nature of warfare. Yet it is hard to be sure, for few people care to admit the guilt they sometimes feel. Possibly the profound aversion to war that is widespread at the mid-century is not entirely due to the political and economic fruitlessness of recent wars and their unprecedented fury. Many who reveal no outward evidence may be aware at some level of their being that the moral issues of war are hardly resolvable on present capital. They may realize that since wars cannot teach nations repentance and humility, they must be abandoned if we are not to lose our inherited humanistic culture. Cut loose from traditional ties, *Homo furens* is seen to be too exclusively devoted to the devastation of the natural and human soil on which he has hitherto been nourished.

If guilt is not experienced deeply enough to cut into us, our future may well be lost. Possibly more people realize this than I suspect; and veterans who did not show any traces of it as warriors may now be feeling it keenly. At all events, there are some who have made that secret journey within the conscience and are building their lives on principles very different from those they knew as unawakened ones.

The Ache of Guilt

Last night I lay awake and thought of all the inhumanity of it, the beastliness of the war. . . . I remembered all the brutal things I had seen since I came overseas, all the people rotting in jail, some of whom I had helped to put there. . . . I thought of Plato's phrase about the wise man caught in an evil time who refuses to participate in the crimes of his fellow citizens, but hides behind a wall until the storm is past. And this morning when I rose, tired and distraught from bed, I knew that in order to survive this time I must love more. There is no other way. . . . (War journal, December 8, 1944)

THE

FUTURE

OF WAR

Today we return to the front! A great change of mood has come over us all. . . . Peace is in sight, or the illusion of peace. And we spring forward in the hope that there will be no more weary winters to spend on war-torn fronts. (War journal, July 6, 1944)

There is in many today as great a fear of a sterile and unexciting peace as of a great war. We are often puzzled by our continued failure to enlist in the pursuit of a peaceful world the unified effort, cheerfulness in sacrifice, determination, and persistence that arise almost spontaneously in the pursuit of war. Rarely do we like to face the ultimate explanations of this fact. The majority of us, restless and unfulfilled, see no supreme worth in our present state. We want more out of life than we are getting and are always half-ready to chance everything on the realization of great expectations. Though most of

215

us do not know what we expect of life, we reject inwardly the fate present existence has in store for us: isolation, petty routines, the stale entrapments society sets for us. Reality is so different from our dreams and the confident hopes of our youth. Happiness is so elusive, won by the privileged few alone. It is this crushing disappointment of our confident expectations that makes us welcome a chance to exercise the military virtues, to escape into adventure, to feel the genuine excitement of the communal and the sacrificial.

If by some magic all the peoples of the world could be assured of eternal peace, a discerning observer would detect genuine regret and disappointment, mingled, of course, with heartfelt sighs of relief and joy.

I confess that in my adolescence and early manhood, before World War II, I longed for one more war, in which I might participate. Though I never spoke of such a wish, and regard it today with considerable dismay, I cannot deny that it was an important part of the aspirations of my youth. And I have no reason to believe that my case is unique or singular. These secret impulses cannot be disregarded. The ways of peace have not found—perhaps cannot find—substitutes for the communal enthusiasms and ecstasies of war. Unless we find a way to change men's hearts, there appears to be small chance that they will fall out of love with destructive violence.

In 1955 I talked with a Frenchwoman who had suffered cruelly during the war from lack of food and anxieties for her family, but was now living in comfortable bourgeois fashion with her husband and son. We reviewed the misadventures of those war days, and then she confessed to me with great earnestness that, despite everything, those times had been more satisfying than the present. "My life is so unutterably boring nowadays!" she cried out. "Anything is better than to have nothing at all happen day after day. You know that I do not love war or want it to return. But at least it made me feel alive, as I have not felt alive before or since."

And a few days later I listened to a strikingly similar report from a German friend. Overweight, and with an expensive cigar in his mouth, he spoke of our earlier days together at the close of the war, when he was shivering and hungry and harried with anxieties about keeping his wife and children from too great want. "Sometimes I think that those were happier times for us than these," he concluded, and there was something like despair in his eyes. Neither one of these people was accustomed to such a confession; it came from both spontaneously and because I had known them in distress and in prosperity. They were not longing for the old days in sentimental nostalgia; they were confessing their disillusionment with a sterile present. Peace exposed a void in them that war's excitement had enabled them to keep covered up.

Violence has been, I think, a perennial refuge from this painful malady. It is hard to overestimate the extent to which millions in our day feed upon violence and the threat of violence for their emotional nourishment. Magazines, newspapers, movies, and television afford a kind of vicarious satisfaction of this appetite. And potential violence is apparent everywhere, in relations of parents and children, of workers and their employers, of racial minorities and majorities within society, and many others. Though organized state violence, which is the definition of war, is different from these, they are hardly separable, for without the secret love of violence and the accustoming of the psyche to it, which daily experience provides, effective fighting in war would be unthinkable.

Sometimes it takes penetrating eyes to notice the violent undercurrents of daily life in our Western society, so commonplace do they seem and so adept are public officials in keeping the more overt out of sight. One can live in Germany, for example, and be impressed with the harmlessness of social life. Underneath the surface, however, slumber volcanic forces no less restless than in previous decades of this century. Violence remains, in the most subtle recesses of the cultural life of this people, a dominant principle. The situation in other countries of Europe, old and tradition-dominated as they are, is only better in degree, if at all. Nor is it at all different in our own land. Given the unfavorable circumstances to which most of these countries have been subjected, we would be appalled at the sinister and brutal forces our country could spawn overnight. What happened under the Nazis in Germany might well serve as an object lesson to all of us for a century to come. Every nation, I believe, conceals in itself violent criminal forces, waiting only for an opportunity to appear in daylight.

Most sobering of all to me is the realization my experience has forced upon me that suffering has very limited power to purge and purify; with the vast majority it is as likely to deteriorate the character and will, or, at best, to leave no lasting mark for good or ill. A theoretical observer might have believed that the anguish of two world wars in a half-century would have guaranteed a mood of repentance and reform, freeing the next decades at least from the pride and arrogance of nations. It has not worked out that way. Suffering appears to improve characters already strong and sensitizes consciences already awake; with others it produces most often the opposite effect.

In Württemberg near the close of the war our division overran a concentration camp which had been recently emptied of inmates and guards. It turned out that the prisoners had been hastily pushed into a string of freight cars and carried as far

218

into the interior of Germany as possible before the guards abandoned them. Our troops came upon them, opened the doors of the freight cars, and allowed the starving band to straggle into the nearest town, where the shocked citizenry took up the task of nursing and caring for them. I spent one long day in their midst and learned a few lessons about human nature in extreme situations I shall not soon forget.

In their condition, glances were more eloquent than words, and an extra pound of flesh on the bones, slightly more color in the cheeks, told more plainly than denunciations could who the oppressors within the camp had been. Like all the concentration camps, this one contained men of a dozen nationalities and social strata, imprisoned anti-Nazis, Jews, captured soldiers, and, as always, a few professional criminals, transferred from penitentiaries to prey upon the others and thus make the guards' task an easier one. The only ones of the group physically strong, these criminals were looked upon by the liberated men with unutterable hatred. Only their emaciation and weakness prevented the inmates from tearing to pieces the oppressors, who had been, by unanimous testimony, worse than the Nazi guards. Never have I seen more evil eyes than these I looked into during questioning. Though these eyes burned with rage and contempt, there was fear, too, and I had the impression that most of the criminals were probably relieved to be made prisoners by us and quickly separated from the rest.

I noticed at once that all the others rallied around one man, who was praised extravagantly as one who had held them together against guards and internal traitors, had preserved their courage and dignity, and become a natural leader over the long months and years. When Frenchmen, of whom there were many of education and position in the camp, lauded this man,

I was astonished to learn that he was a German, a political prisoner of long standing and a veteran of many concentration camps. I spent several hours in conversation with him and discovered a man in whom deprivation had accomplished that rare thing, a cleansing of all hatred and revenge from his heart, leaving him almost uncannily sane and wise. At my request, he outlined his ideas of what should happen in postwar Germany and Europe, and I was as overwhelmed by the moderation of his proposals for punishing our political foes as by the practicality of his positive economic and governmental programs. Here was that man among ten thousand, more accurately, perhaps, among a million, who had used dreadful experiences as means for advancement of his knowledge and compassion. After a few hours with him I understood why all the inmates, even those who hated with passion everything German, spoke of him and to him with unconcealed veneration.

The whole range of human character seemed to be exhibited there by these few hundred survivors during the first day of their liberation, and I was conscious of having stumbled onto an hour of truth that would hardly be repeated, even by them, in later days. There was for me in addition a kind of dread portent of the future in the final words I had with their leader. As I rose to leave, I asked him what he intended to do in the immediate future. "Look for my family," he answered. "My wife has been in concentration camps almost as long as I, and I fear she is long since dead. My two boys were taken by the SS as slave laborers to build fortifications in France and I have reason to hope they are still living, somewhere in Europe. My first task is to try to locate them, as soon as I am strong enough to travel."

The vision of this ravaged man wandering over Europe in

search of his scattered family, possibly finding his youngsters alive but debauched by their associates, revealed one face of future war that will be altogether intolerable. I had already observed that the bitterest of all experiences for European soldiers of World War II was to return to desecrated home towns and to families brutalized by even worse experiences than their own. With thousands of other American soldiers, I had breathed a prayer of thankfulness that the homes we were returning to were not like these. It was a good fortune hardly to be repeated in the future. Now, in retrospect, no change in the character of warfare seems as crucial as this modern blurring of all distinctions between combatants and noncombatants. What this means in terms of moral degradation experiences like this one just described showed me in clearest focus. With civilians and soldiers alike physically and spiritually displaced after future wars, who will be available to heal the sick, the dispirited, and the lost?

Though there is widespread fear that our century in its second half cannot afford or endure a resumption of the warfare that marred the first fifty years, there seems to be little assurance that any secure way has been found to avoid it. Some still quote fatalistically the Biblical lines about wars and rumors of wars, and repeat, as men have done from time immemorial, that because there have always been wars, wars will continue forever, that human nature never changes, that bellicosity is part of man's nature and we cannot therefore eradicate war. Others maintain that another world war is unthinkable because war is no longer, as it was until recently, an instrument of foreign policy. "The rocket and hydrogen bombs are forcing us to grow up," concludes one current report whose author optimistically asserts that "we are further

from world war than we have ever been before in my lifetime."
Then he adds lightly, but with a note of hysteria, often detectable nowadays: "If I am proved wrong on this point no
reader of these lines will be able to expose me, for both he and
I will be dead."

The difficulty of prophecy lies in our inability to discover
what has really changed in the present situation and what only
appears to be changed. At a superficial level, optimism and
pessimism are equally inane. Optimists who base their beliefs
on the ground that modern weapons promise annihilation of
whole peoples and so render any hope of victory for one side
illusory forget, I think, that this situation is hardly permanent.
Under the conditions of whirlwind advance typical of our age,
how can anyone know what possibilities for defense, for
neutralization of great weapons, or what selective destruction
of military and industrial potentialities another decade will
bring forth? And if an ultimate Armageddon does not lie in
the future, who can be sure that a series of limited wars fought
with more conventional weapons will not destroy our civilization, less dramatically but no less thoroughly? So long as
there is no change in the will to warfare, it seems the sheerest
folly to trust, as many now want to do, to the deterrent power
of fear and armed might. In our present state of mind, these
are probably necessary, but they should delude no one into
believing there is any security in the present condition.

If wars begin in the minds of men, it would be wise to
search there for a basis of optimism. And there is, in fact, one
change that appears to be novel and important—our growing
unwillingness to glorify war and the military virtues. In the
literature of battle, there is a decreasing tendency to justify
war in terms of the heroic deeds it calls forth, to romanticize
its grandeur and exalt its personal sacrifices. No longer do we

222

in the West thrill so much to the sentiments of Horace that it is sweet and noble to die for country. Nor do so many of us adhere to the belief, once so widespread, that wars correspond to the will of God. Whether this change is due to the altered nature of war or to a change in the nature of warriors, I am not sure. But I do find a marked lessening of martial appetite among the writers of the twentieth century.

It would be easy to cite pages of encomiums on warfare in the nineteenth century, using German authors, as is usually done. But here is one from our own Oliver Wendell Holmes, Jr., veteran of our Civil War, extreme enough for all and hardly untypical. Who of us today would adhere to the doctrine he wrote as a mature man of fifty-four: "War when you are at it is horrible and dull, it is only when time has passed that you see that its message was divine." Who today would experience anything but disbelief when he continues:

I do not know what is true. I do not know the meaning of the universe. But in the midst of doubt, in the collapse of creeds, there is one thing I do not doubt, that no man who lives in the same world with most of us can doubt, and that is that the faith is true and adorable which leads a soldier to throw away his life in obedience to a blindly accepted duty, in a cause which he little understands, in a plan of campaign of which he has no notion, under tactics of which he does not see the use.

There may well be those who still subscribe to such a faith; in fact, almost certainly some exist in every nation. But it is a safe guess that fewer exist in our decade than formerly, and perhaps a reasonable prophecy that their numbers will steadily decline, despite the fact that more men are under arms than ever before. In this change of mentality, if it be one, there is surely more promise than in any balance of terror.

On the other hand, it must not blind us to the negative elements in the present situation or make us forget the things that have not changed. Too many of us no longer glorify war, I fear, not because we have renounced the deeds of war but because we find our military past inexplicable and dissociated from the present. After a few years of peace we are unable to believe in war and work out excellent reasons to show why it cannot possibly recur. How difficult to realize that so many of the men we brush against every day on the street have killed and maimed other men. So innocent and harmless do we appear, we veterans. We do not glory in this past, to be sure, but that does not destroy its actuality. It requires only a moment's reflection to convince us of the titanic forces that lie beneath the surface of our quiet days. Let us remember how quickly most of us adapted to the logic of combat. Was it not a direct verification of the Freudian theory of reversion to an earlier, primitive personality, which remains intact in the subconscious, unmodified by our later, more sophisticated selves?

A tragic fact of our day, which outweighs all others, in my judgment, is simply this: At a time when the most revolutionary demands are made upon us for conversion to a better form of existence, we are so little ready for any inner change. Few serious students of our society would have the temerity to assert that Western man is more at home in the world now than formerly, any less anxious, or more in charge of his institutions and the larger forces of history. Indeed, most agree that contemporary civilization in America and Europe is unfulfilling in so many ways. Impersonality, monotony, standardization, the scramble to consume and to achieve material comfort induce at times a measureless ennui and the longing for an escape no matter how dangerous and violent.

. . .

224

If optimism and pessimism have become increasingly irrelevant in our terrible dilemma, there is great reason nonetheless to practice the ancient virtue of hope. Though generally
neglected in recent centuries, when optimism about progress
was the rule, hope is that quality of character and virtue of
mind which is directed toward the future in trust rather than
in confidence. Its trust is that human beings will ultimately
prove capable, to the extent granted to mortals, of controlling
their own destinies through reason and wisdom. Poor as the
present outlook for peace is, we can take hope in the realization, coming more and more to be accepted, that nothing except ourselves prevents us from consigning wars to the unhappy past. They correspond neither to God's will nor to the
dictates of necessity.

It was one of the most discouraged thinkers who wrote the
most hopeful of all paragraphs about a future warless world.
His prophecy ought to be regarded as recognition of man's
power to alter the course of events by undergoing an inner
change. I refer, curiously enough, to Friedrich Nietzsche and
to the following paragraph from *The Wanderer and His
Shadow:*

And perhaps the great day will come when a people, distinguished by wars and victories and by the highest development of
a military order and intelligence, and accustomed to make the
heaviest sacrifice for these things, will exclaim of its own free
will, "we break the sword," and will smash its military establish-
ment down to its lowest foundations. *Rendering oneself unarmed
when one has been the best armed,* out of a height of feeling—
that is the means to real peace, which must always rest on a peace
of mind; whereas the so-called armed peace, as it now exists in
all countries, is the absence of peace of mind. One trusts neither
oneself nor one's neighbor and, half from hatred, half from fear,
does not lay down arms. Rather perish than hate and fear, and

twice rather perish than make oneself hated and feared—this must someday become the highest maxim for every single commonwealth too.

This is surely one of the most remarkable prophecies in Western literature. Nietzsche rightly sees that war-making must be overcome through strength and voluntary decision of a strong nation or group of nations; peace will never occur as a consequence of weakness, exhaustion, or fear. Just as the destructive lusts within us require superior power for their containment, so does an institution as deeply rooted in our society as is war require strength for its eradication. A peace of the peoples is hardly something that will steal over us unawares. Prepared for by a gradual change in the disposition of dominant groups, the final stroke will come in consequence of a daring, voluntary, and decisive act of breaking the sword. That can happen only when strength of mind and resolution of will no longer feel the need of external supports like prestige and protocol. It can happen even then only when a nation "out of a height of feeling" takes the decision to risk everything for a supreme good.

This is the second point of importance that Nietzsche makes. In addition to moral strength, courage will be needed, and that of the rarest kind, if war is to be extirpated from our race. The strong are, unfortunately, not always the brave, particularly not when they must expose themselves to the threat of the less strong. How exceedingly unlikely that any of the world's stronger nations today would have the courage to disarm before their enemies! Only a few pacifists have the temerity to suggest such a thing. Who among our political leaders is strong enough to take the responsibility for an act like this? Many might say: "If I had myself alone to answer for, it would be worth the risk. But what right have I to jeopardize

future generations of my people by so irrevocable an act as
this? Individuals can afford to take their lives in their hands;
rulers must tread the cautious path of security. As the people's
representative, my duty is to guarantee their safety as best I
can for the short time they are under my care. Dreamers and
utopians are fit for writing books; they have no function in
responsible political office."

This is the wisdom of the world today, and woe betide the
ruler who does not follow it. The vast majority of our people
want our "armed peace" no less than their representatives, or,
more correctly, they see no alternative to a peace of armed
might. The other path is too beset with risks, and the implicit
rule appears to be: Better to perish through caution than
through folly. Nevertheless, there have been, in rare moments
of world history, intellectual and political leaders who have
persuaded their people to take risks nearly as momentous as
this would be. They have been all too few, of course, and of
these few most have failed. Yet nearly all that is best in our
cultural heritage is traceable to their courage and resolution.

One day in the ripeness of time new leaders may appear
who will induce their peoples to take the irrevocable step, an
act so bold it will be greatly contagious and compel imitation.
Obviously such a deed will not be wholly the work of one man
or a small group. The people as a whole must be ready to
support the act. But even when large numbers have undergone
that inner change of mind and heart described in earlier chapters, it will still require the most courageous of leaders to
break the sword in their name and thus assume responsibility
for possible failure. A man will be needed of great simplicity
and profound conviction.

The most important point of all in Nietzsche's prophecy is
a necessary motivation for breaking the sword. If permanent

227

peace is ever to come over the world, it will be made possible only by motives that are hardly yet operative in political life. "Rather perish than hate and fear, and twice rather perish than make oneself hated and feared." If the rank and file of a great nation could accept a statement of this kind, our future might be assured. Most of us do not enjoy hating and fearing political enemies, but we prefer it infinitely to perishing. We prefer it even when we realize that, indulged in to an extreme degree, hating and fearing destroy our humanity and make us little better than beasts.

If so many of us did not prefer life on almost any terms, we should recognize how intolerable are the burdens of fear and hate which oppress us in our time. They induce us to spend the greater part of our national substance on arms and armor, thereby depriving our people of much-needed schools, hospitals, libraries, and a thousand other benefits of organized political life. Hate and fear impel us to propagandize our youth, to twist and torment the truth into national and provincial molds instead of allowing it the universal frame it requires. Hate and fear narrow our sympathies, choke back our generous impulses, make us caricatures of our possible selves. When one considers these things and many more that might be mentioned in any just indictment of hate and fear, there need be no surprise that any free spirit would prefer perishing to life under their dominion.

However, the more important reason for breaking the sword, says Nietzsche—and he is surely right—is that men ought to choose death twice in preference to being feared and hated. Until this becomes the highest maxim for a commonwealth, as it is now for exceptional individuals, we shall not have reached our goal. Such an impractical motive may on first hearing astonish us, so contrary to our natural impulses is it, and may occasion a contemptuous smile on the faces of so-called realistic men of the world. Why should a nation resolve to be no longer feared and hated and be willing to pay any price for such a resolution?

The answer is terribly hard to give to worldly minds who like to calculate advantages and measure motives as they measure materials. They will hardly comprehend a decision made by Socrates many hundred years ago to suffer injustice in preference to committing it because the former did less harm to the soul. The reason a nation that seeks to be just must abhor being hated and feared is not very different. To hate and fear are evil and damaging to our inner life, but being hated and feared are still more destructive of our higher impulses and potentialities. Nothing corrupts our soul more surely and more subtly than the consciousness of others who fear and hate us. Such is our human nature that we cannot possess power that others dread without becoming like the image of their fear and hate. To possess dread power does not corrupt us overnight; our features may remain benign for years. But inevitably the awareness that others tremble or grow enraged at sight of us poisons the mind and makes us, individuals or nations, in the end into aggressive pariahs, distrustful, capricious, and empty.

If nations ever reach the moral heights attained by exceptional individuals, they will shudder at the images of themselves their neighbors harbor. And they will do everything thinkable to change these images. The image of itself that a strong and gentle nation will one day find most intolerable is of a colossus, jealous of its prestige and alert to pounce upon any who challenge the established order. Conscious of its own intentions and motives, such a nation will not rest until others are aware of those intentions too. This can be accomplished only by deeds that cost something, not by words no matter how eloquent. Whatever the cost, the strong and gentle nation will bend every effort to close the gap between what it is and what it seems to others to be, for the cleft between seeming and being is a fatal one for the nation that is intent on reformation. A strong and gentle nation can only realize its aims when others are fully aware that power and gentleness can coexist and become the greatest benison for an unhappy world.

Nietzsche's prophecy declares that war must be ended suddenly, by a stroke that leaves no one in doubt about the significance of the deed. As the context of the paragraph quoted makes clear, Nietzsche believes that no gradualism can succeed here. On the contrary, men will have to make someday an absolute break with their past, as dope addicts must with their habit, if war is to pass away. The problem of war is no ordinary one, to be combated and resolved like other social issues. It demands an emotional reorientation of such a kind that men will thenceforth date their liberation from that day. In Biblical language, this transformation will be apocalyptic in kind, comparable to the ancient command of the Lord: Let there be light! Afterward, men will be unable to comprehend how it was they could have lived in darkness. "Let us break the sword," someone will declare, in effect, and out of a heightened feeling men will respond by destroying the engines of destruction and will resolve to learn the ways of war no longer.

There is no doubt that practical men will scoff at such a prophecy, contrary as it is to acceptable procedure of our time and to the course of most previous history. Moreover, the statesmen and internationalists who are laboring earnestly in the United Nations and elsewhere to forge little by little the fragile chains of peace are likely to consider the notion of a sudden end of war by an act of national will a foolish and dangerous dream.

To be sure, it would be an irresponsible man who would suggest that we give up the hard work of our international agencies in order to wait for something so uncertain and unreliable as a popular response of the sort Nietzsche suggests. What we need to do without fail is to redouble our efforts in international affairs, seeking the development of retarded areas, searching for legal justice in international disputes, and placating national resentments through resort to conferences and all the arts of compromise. If through these means we can extend one by one the years of our present uneasy peace, wars can be made to seem more outmoded sociologically, economically, and politically than they already do. Even if much of the effort of our international agencies does not directly promote the cause of world peace, it is desirable in its own right and must be done. Peace is, after all, not the only end that men legitimately pursue, and no one really knows in many instances what does contribute to peace in the long run.

Granting all this, I am nonetheless convinced that a transformation of a deep-going inner sort will have to come over men before war can be vanquished. All the machinery of international diplomacy and the highest standard of living for retarded peoples cannot bring about this change. It may be poetic exaggeration to assert that this conversion will happen suddenly; what is meant is that it will be a decisive change. In earlier chapters I have described it as an awakening, a coming to oneself, a discovery of friendship, a falling in love. Human nature, the ultimate source of all hostility, must be converted from its present state of hatred and fear in order to liberate powers within us the existence of which is suspected only by the tiny minority. Neither governments nor other institutions are able to combat at present the destructive forces latent within most of us. The leaders we need are not likely to spring from the earth; they, too, require for success a change in the populace of a fundamental kind.

How must we change, if there is ever to be opportunity to break the sword once and for all? The question is as difficult as it is suggestive and seductive. The temptation to forsake the bounds of the probable is great, but all of us are weary of socialist utopias which describe men who have unlearned customary pleasures, needs, and desires. Realistically, we should not expect men to alter their outer manner of life at all drastically, for changes can be thorough and revolutionary with comparatively little external reformation. The deepest changes of all are indeed likely to return us to the workaday world outwardly little affected, though our actions now proceed from a different motivation and eventually reshape the human environment.

The ancient Greek philosopher Heracleitus once wrote that "men are estranged from what is most familiar and they must seek out what is in itself evident." The sentence illuminates, as few others have done, much of my own war experience. The atmosphere of violence draws a veil over our eyes, preventing us from seeing the plainest facts of our daily existence. To an awakened conscience, everything about human actions becomes then strange and nearly inexplicable. Why men fight without anger and kill without compunction is understandable at all only to a certain point. A slight alteration in consciousness would be sufficient to put their deeds in a true light and turn them forever from destruction. It would require only a coming to themselves to transform killers into friends and lovers, for, paradoxical as it may seem, the impulses that make killers are not so different in kind from those that make lovers. I know no other explanation for the notorious linkage in war between the noblest and the basest deeds, the most execrable vices and the sublimest virtues.

The feeling of being at home in the world is likewise not much removed from the feeling of being exposed and hopelessly lost to all succor. And the sense of being thrown into being that existentialist thinkers describe is removed only by a line from the experience of man created in God's image that was painted by Michelangelo in the wonderful fresco "The Creation of Man." The change in us from the one state of being to the other is, of course, profound, but the psychological distance to traverse is slight. Most of us have known both extremes, often in an incredibly short span of time. It is as though a thin but impenetrable wall separated the two states. If at moments the wall seems easily torn away, usually it proves to be more durable than our lives.

Hence the search for that most familiar and evident of all truths, the belonging together of the human species, in religious terms, the brotherhood of man, is rarely attended with success. In World War II, I found myself separating those soldiers who were awakened and aware of their situation from those who were lost in it. The former were those I could communicate with and understand; the others were simply "the others," beyond my sympathy and concern. Yet in moments of clarity nothing is more apparent than the fact that the best and the worst of men are different in degree only, not in kind. The soldier who is moved by sentiments of friendship and preservative love can reject the soldier-killer, for example, but he cannot in justice deny common humanity with him. Nor should the soldier of conscience who acknowledges his guilt at every level fail to recognize the potentiality of similar

233

awakening in the most reckless and ruthless of his comrades as well as in the enemy. There is too much evidence of such transformations for any of us to doubt.

The case is hardly otherwise in our present uneasy state of peace. To overcome this alienation from the evident and the familiar we need, above all, a genuine closeness to each other in contrast to the separation and isolation that now prevails so widely. It is evident that the overcoming of physical space is not bringing this nearness. As our planet becomes more and more overcrowded and problems of living space and food grow more pressing, the chances for conflict indeed become greater. Evidently there is little or no relationship between physical and psychical nearness, for it is possible to be alienated from one's own roommate and be near to someone a thousand miles removed in space.

So long as we are far from ourselves, it is impossible to be near to others. Well-meaning people often assume that what is required of us today is a wider set of relationships than is possible within the simple and natural unities of family, town, and province. The typical citizens of Kansas, Brittany, and Formosa can hardly become close to each other in any sense demanding intimate acquaintance with one another. What all of us need to gain is a closer relationship to those immediately about us. He who knows what genuine friendship is or the fullest type of erotic love cannot be as estranged from self or others as they are who have never experienced these things.

This nearness to each other, even if it be with one other human being, promotes greatly the development of reflection and self-awareness. Persons who know intimacy are driven to put the important questions: Who am I? Why am I? What is to be my function in life? The kind of knowledge they seek is not of a subtle kind, commonly miscalled philosophical, which an untutored man could not be expected to have. On the contrary, it is this knowledge that people of little formal learning are frequently pursuing more avidly than the falsely sophisticated. Because they are concerned with the important questions, they sometimes achieve the important gift of simplicity. I know of no better way to reach the familiar and the evident than by stripping away superfluities in our emotional, reflective, and social selves, and in our external environment as well. Simplicity manifests itself in directness of approach to other human beings, in the absence of dissembling and guile. Knowing himself, the simple man is conscious that the man he is addressing is, in essentials, not different from himself, and it is the human being in the other that he insists on speaking to.

A condition of this intimacy, all too rarely recognized by most of us, is a different attitude toward the objects of nature around us. A habit of intimacy with the things of nature can fan the creative sparks within us and strengthen the concern for preserving ourselves and others. It is not a misty sentimental feeling for nature writ large that we require; but, rather, a recognition of our dependence on the most humble objects of everyday use and of their importance and place in existence. Until we learn to experience more simply and directly our gardens and trees, the skies above us, and all the objects amid which we move and work, we will find it difficult to achieve closeness to neighbors and even to ourselves.

I have become convinced that the familiar and the evident are so remote because we moderns have increasingly separated ourselves from nature by replacing a primary artistic response to things with a technological mentality. Contrary to the will of many scientists, our science has become much too often an instrument for the exploitation of things and people. We have become so preoccupied with power and control over nature that we have lost an important dimension of our being, the disposition of thankfulness, of commemoration, of perceiving and enjoying something for its own sake. Instead of viewing these immediate objects of our environment in terms of their own being, we have come to regard them solely in terms of what they are for us. And to such an exploitative mentality, nature's voice becomes mute. Approached as material merely, to be worked up and pressed into the service of a self-styled lord of creation, she contains no revelation and no blessing.

To the man who is not interested in what a thing is in itself and for itself, no intimate relations are possible. Nature can be infinitely abused by such a one, but by no means understood. Only the cherishing, object-centered eye of the artist latent in all of us can make and keep us aware that nature does not exist only for us, but in her own right as well. The artistic gaze alone can discern those qualities in nature that are able to heal our restlessness and overcome our boredom, by enhancing the value of the commonplace. Art can reconcile us to our individual and collective fates as nothing else can, except perhaps religion. But art (I do not speak of the fine arts) has declined in our society as the narrow utilitarian ideal has grown, and the results are lamentable.

The effect on our religious traditions of this appropriative, ego-centered disposition of mind has been hardly less disastrous. Religion, like art, points to something greater and more worthy than the self and impels us to pay it homage. Religion relates man to his origins, aiding him thus in the search for a reason for existence. Modern man finds it hard indeed to discover anything in the universe worthy of worship. More often than not he conceives himself to be at the top of an unordered creation, able to survey the whole and to do with it what he will. But few are ready to worship him; he has demonstrated often enough that he is lacking in divine serenity and endurance.

Moreover, he himself knows full well that he can be no proper god, for he is filled with a longing for something or someone to whom to belong. In the face of an overpowering universe, he realizes, consciously or not, that his freedom and independence are relative and puny. What is missing so often in modern men is a basic piety, the recognition of dependence on the natural realm. And they feel the need of this piety without possessing it. There is no dearth of religions in our time, and they fulfill certain needs, but there is a general absence of religious passion for belonging to an order infinitely transcending the human. Separated from close association with nature and intimacy with her ways, we find it difficult to do homage to nature's god.

This separation of man from nature as a consequence of our too-exclusive interest in power is in part responsible for the total wars of our century. More than we ever realize, we have transferred our exploitative attitudes from nature to man. In total war, men become so much material, and civilian populations, like soldiers, have to be ravaged and subdued. Distinctions between innocent and guilty, the permissible and the prohibited, become extinguished. Men and machines approach each other more nearly. The most painful impressions of World War II for me, as I have said, were the ruthless trampling down of the works of nature and the innocent products of human art. Try as I might, I cannot but recoil, even in memory, from the destructive fury of a modern army directed upon the things of nature and her creatures, all untainted by any partisanship. The butchering of each other was almost

237

easier to endure than the violation of animals, crops, farms, homes, bridges, and all the other things that bind man to his natural environment and help to provide him with a spiritual home.

Since that war, there has been no convincing evidence of change in this exploitative mentality. The fashioning of the atom bomb seems to me too dangerously typical of the modern mind, and the recent experiments with the hydrogen bomb an unrecognized blasphemy. Hardly anyone considers it possible that the poisoning of fish in the ocean by these experiments might be worthy of condemnation. Man can sin only against man, it seems, or possibly against God, not against nature. That the ocean should be violated, a region hitherto relatively immune from destructive lusts, seems to most, apparently, nothing else than a triumph of natural science.

In the desperate state of human relations in our day, one can understand the argument for testing weapons in order to keep national defenses strong. But I am objecting to the spirit in which it is done, involving, as it does, indifference to all that is not of human origin or use. This lack of concern stands, I believe, as a great barrier to the elimination of war. Before expecting man to spare his brother, we must persuade him to spare those things around him that contribute to his life as greatly as his brothers do. The growth of that preservative love and care which is in strongest opposition to destructive lusts involves an intimacy with things of which too many of us have as yet hardly an inkling.

The gift of nearness to the familiar and evident is happiness. Whatever else is true, we in the West will not learn to break the sword until we have happier populations. If there are any laws of psychology in this area at all, one must be that a happy people is a peaceful people. The capacity for happiness which most of us possess receives too rarely the sustenance it needs to become more than a capacity; more often it shrinks as we grow older. The longing for a paradise, which our hearts believe to be possible but which we cannot find, robs us of serenity; the large expectations of our youth remain unfulfilled. Though the components of happiness are no doubt many and not the same for all, emotional and intellectual intimacy with others is surely the one component essential to nearly all of us. For the few, association with the things of nature can of itself produce a happiness that suffices to fulfill the more solitary members of our species. But, for the majority, nearness to the things of daily existence can be a means for entering into closeness with other human beings, whether it be the comradeship of labor, the partnership of marriage, the friendship of kindred minds, or other associations.

More than anything else, happiness can provide a secure bottom to the world, sufficient to persuade us that we are no accidents on this planet. Happiness alone can transform the dull and colorless daily scene into an order pregnant with meaning and delight. When a person finds a friend to whom he can open his heart, when a woman finds a man she can love and to whom she can bear children, when any of us find a community we can love and serve, our little lives take on a significance we had not dreamed of. Far from being the restless ones who welcome war as a possible path to forbidden experience, we experience the threat of war as completely intolerable. Those who have a stake in peace realize too well that war can occasion the loss of all.

Nations containing genuinely happy citizens would shrink from exposing their great fortunes to the cruel chances of combat far more than wealthy nations now shun war from fear of loss. More than this, a nation with happy citizens would encounter greater difficulty in maintaining a hostile disposition in themselves or others, since happiness always presses toward universality. The people who one day break with their military past and declare that they no longer can endure to be hated and feared will not only be a happy people; their deed will be largely a result of their happiness. Having experienced closeness to each other, they will be eager to extend the experience to others. And for this they may be willing to take the greatest risks, more trustful and of larger faith than we.

I have often meditated on my chance meeting with the old hermit in Italy, and have tried to puzzle out why he impressed me so much. Perhaps it was not only his ignorance of the war and my inability to explain why we were fighting, but also certain qualities I sensed in him which were in starkest contrast with my own state. What these qualities were it is still not easy for me to name exactly. Born on a farm and brought up with country people, as I have been, I am wary of sentimentalizing the old man of the mountain. I have no doubt he possessed the ordinary human quota of meanness, dishonesty, and avarice. He and his hermit kind can obviously do little for the peace of the world now or in any conceivable future. But there was about him a rare peaceableness and sanity that I have slowly come to associate with a better, peaceful world.

Though he had probably never seen an American in his life, he welcomed me beside him on the grass, and I have never felt less like an intruder in my life. Despite the handicap of language, we began to talk at once of important things as naturally as if we knew one another well. There was no strangeness about our meeting, our talk, or our parting, though the experience as a whole was the strangest one of the war for me.

I felt in him the strength of his close association with the things of nature. The serenity in his eyes, voice, and movements was not the dullness of the lout or vacant-minded. Even if he had lived through none of the storms more sensitive and gifted people experience, he seemed to possess a constancy, patience, and endurance not often known to them. I could not guess and did not ask what his history had been and why he had chosen this life, but it was clear that he had gained a kind of wisdom from solitude which enabled him to live simply and happily. In fact, he appeared to be singularly at home in the world, as though he had sprung from nature herself and thought of himself as her authentic child. Harmless and wise and innocent, he dwelt here in the mountains, ready to chat with all who chanced by and to ask them anew about those strange and infernal noises in the valley which he would never understand. When a large number of people become, like him, truly unable to understand why nations war with one another, the human species will no longer be in mortal danger of extinction.

Possibly his gentleness and simplicity had taught him, too, not to exaggerate the significance of the human story in relation to the rest of nature's household. At least watching the stars at night, as soldiers often have to do on lonely guard duty or in their foxholes, can rob one of the arrogance that makes men believe their history is the beginning and end of the things that are. After my visit with the old man, I drew comfort from the words of Plato: "Think you . . . that the little affairs of men here below are of great interest to the God who reigns over all."

Far from making a man sad and defeatist, this perspective

241

can instil a kind of serenity. The larger purposes of the universe, though far transcending our weak powers of comprehension, may, after all, not be dependent on the history of man. If we are not the chief end of creation, as assuredly we are not, the whole in which we are included as a small sum may have meaning and purpose. Though man's wars may be too small from a cosmic vista for any pattern to be descried, they may, nevertheless, be purposeful enough if one could see events with less myopic vision than we possess. In any case, it is time that we human beings abandoned the overweening faith that only through us can the objectives of creation be realized. That faith needs to be replaced by the confidence that, even if we vanish from the earth sooner or later as a consequence of our failures, that, too, will be within the compass of a Being incomparably greater and more enduring than the race of man.

About this last there is for me an impenetrable mystery, as there is about the nature of man himself. War reveals dimensions of human nature both above and below the acceptable standards for humanity. In the end, any study of war must strive to deal with gods and devils in the form of man. It is recorded in the holy scriptures that there was once war in heaven, and the nether regions are still supposed to be the scene of incessant strife. Interpreted symbolically, this must mean that the final secrets of why men fight must be sought beyond the human, in the nature of being itself.